Unsung Heroines

35 Women Who Changed the Bay Area

RAE ALEXANDRA

ILLUSTRATED BY ADRIENNE SIMMS

CITY LIGHTS FOUNDATION

CITY LIGHTS / SAN FRANCISCO

COVER DESIGN BY JEFF MELLIN
INTERIOR DESIGN BY VICTOR MINGOVITS

LIBRARY OF CONGRESS CATALOGING-IN-PUBLICATION DATA
NAMES: ALEXANDRA, RAE AUTHOR | SIMMS, ADRIENNE ILLUSTRATOR
TITLE: UNSUNG HEROINES: 35 WOMEN WHO CHANGED THE BAY AREA / BY RAE ALEXANDRA; ILLUSTRATED BY ADRIENNE SIMMS.
IDENTIFIERS: LCCN 2025045381 (PRINT) | LCCN 2025045382 (EBOOK) | ISBN 9781931404204 TRADE PAPERBACK | ISBN 9781931404211 EBOOK
SUBJECTS: LCSH: WOMEN—CALIFORNIA—SAN FRANCISCO BAY AREA—BIOGRAPHY | WOMEN—SOCIAL CONDITIONS—CALIFORNIA—SAN FRANCISCO BAY AREA | WOMEN SOCIAL REFORMERS—CALIFORNIA—SAN FRANCISCO BAY AREA—BIOGRAPHY | SAN FRANCISCO BAY (CALIF.)—HISTORY | LCGFT: BIOGRAPHIES
CLASSIFICATION: LCC CT3262.C25 A44 2026 (PRINT) | LCC CT3262.C25 (EBOOK)
LC RECORD AVAILABLE AT HTTPS://LCCN.LOC.GOV/2025045381
LC eBOOK RECORD AVAILABLE AT HTTPS://LCCN.LOC.GOV/2025045382

CITY LIGHTS FOUNDATION BOOKS ARE PUBLISHED AT THE
CITY LIGHTS BOOKSTORE,
261 COLUMBUS AVENUE,
SAN FRANCISCO, CA 94133.

WWW.CITYLIGHTS.COM

"A newspaper by and for Indigenous people. Immigrants and their descendants allowed to marry Americans. Free public toilets for women. Voting by mail. Saving the San Francisco Bay. Children getting breakfast. Children with disabilities attending school. Care for people with AIDS. Health centers. All this and more. The Bay Area would not be as civilized as it is without the brave work of the women in this book. At last, we can know them, and sing their praises." — **MAXINE HONG KINGSTON, AUTHOR OF *THE WOMAN WARRIOR: MEMOIRS OF A GIRLHOOD AMONG GHOSTS***

"Fascinating, engaging, thorough, thoughtful, and surprising, *Unsung Heroines* is an absolute treasure trove of just some of the rad women who've shaped the Bay Area and Northern California—and the nation. As a feminist history buff and lifelong Bay Area resident who's done a lot of research on the cool women who came before me, I had never heard of well over half the women profiled in this book. I'm so grateful to Rae Alexandra for teaching me—and every reader!—about them. Put this book in every classroom, office, coffeeshop, and BART train! These are stories that every resident of the region needs to know!" — **KATE SCHATZ, AUTHOR OF *RAD AMERICAN WOMEN A-Z***

"Overlooked no more! Alexandra has unearthed the brilliant stories of 35 fascinating Bay Area women. You'll find adventure, inspiration, strength, and wisdom on every page. From the early fighters for racial equality to the Gold Rush-era women who held

their own in rough-and-tumble California, Alexandra illuminates the long-lost stories of women from all walks of life. This worthy collection of biographies offers a more complete history of the Bay Area and early California. A must-read for history buffs. Educational, fascinating, compelling . . . and downright fun."
— OLIVIA ALLEN-PRICE, AUTHOR OF *BAY CURIOUS: EXPLORING THE HIDDEN TRUE STORIES OF THE SAN FRANCISCO BAY AREA*

"Rae Alexandra proves that our greatest source of wealth is our treasure trove of stories about women who created a stir while making positive change in the world. I learned so much from this incredible book, and I gained so much inspiration and fuel for action. You'll never look at Bay Area history the same way again. *Unsung Heroines* is essential reading." **— CHARLIE JANE ANDERS, AUTHOR OF *LESSONS IN MAGIC AND DISASTER***

"Every story here is a unique adventure that reminds us of women's vision and bravery. The evocative portraits by Adrienne Simms make this a real celebration of these daring human rights activists who cross boundaries of time, ethnicity, and class and invite us all to join in." **— JEWELLE GOMEZ, AUTHOR OF *THE GILDA STORIES***

For my mother, Mavis,
without whom this book would not exist.

TABLE OF CONTENTS

INTRODUCTION

This book is the result of an abiding sense of frustration.

When I first started writing the *Rebel Girls From Bay Area History* series for KQED, on which this book is based, I was furious. It was 2018 and I had just found out the percentage of public space afforded to women in San Francisco. At the time, just 12% of the city's street names, statues, parks and public art honored women. As a longtime resident of San Francisco, I knew the names of important men from the city's history. The names of the significant women, however, escaped me entirely.

I knew they were out there somewhere, if only I could figure out where their histories had been buried. I made a pledge to myself that I would find and honor five unsung women on KQED's website for Women's History Month in 2018. It was a simple enough idea. What I hadn't counted on was just how many audacious, brave and irrepressible Bay Area heroines I would discover, starting from the very earliest days of the Gold Rush and marching tenaciously up to the present day. Over the course of seven years, my five profiles slowly expanded to 55. You will find 35 of those women in this book.

I realize now that, told in chronological order, these essays don't just reflect the achievements of exceptional Bay Area women over the past 175 years. They also give an overview of the history and social progress of Northern California itself. Whether their names are widely recognized or not, the actions of these diverse activists, educators, philanthropists, organizers and mavericks have indelibly impacted how we in the Bay Area continue to live today.

Their stories deserve to be heard.

Their names deserve to be known.

May the women you're about to meet inspire you as much as they have inspired me.

a b c
d f
g l
m n

Elizabeth Thorn Scott Flood

ON MAY 29, 1854, a 26-year-old woman opened the doors to her Sacramento home and invited 14 students inside. This simple act — in a humble house on Second Street — established the first private school for African American children in the city.

From these scrappy beginnings, teacher Elizabeth Thorn Scott Flood would go on to change education in Northern California forever.

By the time she opened that first school in Sacramento, Elizabeth had already proven herself incredibly resilient. Two years earlier, she had left New Bedford, Massachusetts, traveling by ship across the Isthmus of Panama and on to California, so that her husband, Joseph Scott — then a mariner — could become a gold miner. Soon after they had settled in the rowdy mining community of Hangtown (now Placerville), Joseph died suddenly, leaving Elizabeth alone with their infant son, Oliver. Understanding that Hangtown was not a safe environment for a single mom, she soon made the move to Sacramento.

A few years later, when Oliver was refused entry to the local public school based on the color of his skin, Elizabeth became determined to open a school. After talking with her equally frustrated neighbors, that determination grew beyond the necessity of educating her own child and toward bettering the lives of her entire community. Some of her first 14 students were adults.

Within three months of opening her home this way, Elizabeth was in need of a larger classroom; children of Asian and Native American descent also wanted to enroll. So she moved classes to Siloam Baptist Chapel and to St. Andrew's Methodist Episcopal Church. Within a year, the Sacramento School Board accepted Elizabeth's school into the official school district, making Elizabeth's the first African American public school in Sacramento. However, the Board refused to provide her with any funding, following the example of the rest of the state. (Although the California Constitutional Convention had introduced a tax fund for state schools in 1849, local school boards routinely granted funding to white schools only.) And so, Elizabeth's students had to agree to pay tuition of one dollar per week to keep her doors open.

Meanwhile, Elizabeth involved herself in civic matters beyond her school. St. Andrew's hosted California's first State Convention of Colored Citizens in November 1855. The convention's primary concerns were voting and housing rights, civil rights protections and access to education. Elizabeth was in attendance, as were 49 delegates from 10 California counties.

That same year, she married Isaac Flood, a man who, unlike Elizabeth, had been born into slavery. Flood had purchased his own freedom and moved to Oakland during the Gold Rush, and, at the time they met, he was working as a tradesman. Flood was also a single parent to a young son, and the merged family soon moved to the area east of Lake Merritt — then named Brooklyn. Elizabeth left her school in the capable hands of another teacher from Massachusetts, Jeremiah B. Sanderson. It was on his watch that a new schoolhouse was finally built for Sacramento's children of color in 1855.

As one of the first African American families to settle in Oakland, the Floods made their presence felt immediately with a series of firsts. In 1857, Elizabeth turned their home into Oakland's first private school for Black children. That same year, the couple conceived their first child together, and George Flood was said to be the first Black baby born in Oakland. The next year, in 1858, the Floods helped establish Oakland's first Black church — the First African Methodist Episcopal Church. When the church moved into a former schoolhouse, Elizabeth taught classes there, too.

In 1866, Elizabeth's fight for better schools began to pay off. Until then, there was no law to protect the right of Black children to attend school. The Revised School Law required the establishment of a public school for Black students in any district with ten or more Black children who wanted to attend, or else make allowances for them to join white schools — as long as the majority of white parents didn't object.

The following year, Elizabeth's campaign for equal education came to a tragic halt when she died suddenly at the age of 39. But her loving husband picked up the baton, later serving as secretary on the Education Committee of the Colored Citizens of California. Crucially, in 1871, he successfully petitioned the Oakland School Board to admit children of color based on the passage of the Fourteenth and Fifteenth Amendments. Finally, in 1880, integrated schools became California law.

Elizabeth and Isaac's youngest child was just five years old when she lost her mother — but she inherited Elizabeth's determination. Lydia Flood Jackson was one of the first children in Oakland to attend a desegregated school, and later went on to campaign for women's suffrage, speaking at the 1918 California State Women's Convention and serving on the board of the Federation of Women's Colored Clubs.

Elizabeth Thorn Scott Flood dedicated her short life to bucking a status quo that refused to serve her people. She decided that the best way to prevail over a system that excluded her was to work outside of it, and she set good example after good example until the system finally caught up. Those who remember her rightfully call her the Mother of Desegregated Education in California. The number of children's lives she transformed is impossible to calculate.

12th District Co
TICKET
FOR ONE TRIP
Charlott L. Brown
J. 136. — vs — 10.588
Omnibus Railroad Co
Copy Complaint

Charlotte L. Brown

TWO YEARS BEFORE SLAVERY was officially abolished by the 13th Amendment, and a full 92 years before Rosa Parks refused to give up her seat on the bus, Charlotte L. Brown took on San Francisco's racially segregated Omnibus Railroad and Cable Company and changed the city's public transportation laws forever.

On April 17, 1863, Charlotte boarded a horse-drawn streetcar, a relatively new form of transport. When the conductor reached her, he refused to take the ticket she had bought and asked her to leave, saying that "colored persons" — two percent of San Francisco's population at the time — were not allowed to ride. Charlotte, in her early 20s at the time, had successfully circumvented streetcar segregation laws many times before, sometimes by wearing a veil. She refused to move. When a white woman joined the conductor in demanding she go, Charlotte was physically removed.

Charlotte was not one to go quietly, however, thanks in large part to the way her tenacious parents had raised her. Her father, James E. Brown, made a living running his own stable, but in his personal life, James was a co-founder of the Bay Area's first African American newspaper, *Mirror of the Times*, and was an outspoken abolitionist rumored to protect fugitive slaves. James had once been a slave himself, released from servitude only when his wife, a seamstress whom Charlotte was named after, had raised enough money to buy his freedom.

Charlotte and her family had moved to San Francisco from Maryland at some point during the 1850s, shortly after slavery was abolished in California. By the time she was forced from that streetcar, the Brown family was living in North Beach and were prominent figures in the local Black community.

Charlotte and her father decided to take action by bringing a lawsuit against Omnibus Railroad, an extraordinarily brave move. When she gave her affidavit, Charlotte spoke plainly:

> I lived one block from where I took the car. When the conductor first came to me and refused to take my ticket, I told him I thought I had a right to ride, it was a public conveyance. I told him I had a long distance to go. . . . I told him I would not get out. . . . He took hold of my arm. I made no resistance. I knew it was of no use to resist and therefore I went out, and he kept hold of me until I was out of the car, holding on to me until I struck the walk.

During the case, Omnibus defended its racist policies, arguing that people of color should not be permitted to ride streetcars in case they made white women and children feel "fearful or repulsed."

While Charlotte ultimately won the case and was awarded $25 and costs, appeals by Omnibus kept her tied up in court for months. The end result saw her award sum reduced to just five cents, the cost of Charlotte's original ticket. What's more, the case did not change Omnibus policy. Shortly after the first case was finally over, Charlotte was removed from another Omnibus streetcar.

Charlotte and her father returned to court, this time finding themselves arguing in front of a sympathetic judge. Judge Orville C. Pratt of the 12th District Court deemed segregation barbaric and, in his landmark 1864 ruling, stated:

> It has been already quite too long tolerated by the dominant race to see with indifference the Negro or mulatto treated as a brute, insulted, wronged, enslaved, made to wear a yoke, to tremble before white men, to serve him as a tool, to hold property and life at his will, to surrender to

> him his intellect and conscience, and to seal his lips and belie his thought through dread of the white man's power.

Charlotte was awarded $500.

She continued to follow in the footsteps of her fierce family later in life. A decade after winning her court case, Charlotte married fellow activist James Henry Riker, who was one of the organizers of the 1865 California State Convention of Colored Citizens, which brought together Black activists, churches, social clubs and literary societies to plan courses of action. The couple stayed in San Francisco, where Charlotte established a primary school in North Beach.

It's possible that Charlotte's case bolstered Mary Ellen Pleasant in 1866 when she, more famously, brought a lawsuit against North Beach and Mission Railroad Company for forcing her from a streetcar, an ongoing problem for San Francisco's Black population for years after Charlotte's case concluded. Pleasant's lawsuit made it all the way to California's Supreme Court, and in 1893, a statewide ban on streetcar segregation finally came into effect.

Jumberlie
A Creole Dish

Take one chicken and cut it up, separating every joint and adding to it one pint of cleanly washed rice. Take about half a dozen large tomatoes, scalding them well and taking the skins off with a knife. Cut them in small pieces and put them with the chicken in a pot or arge porcelain saucepan

Abby Fisher

IN 1870s SAN FRANCISCO, once Abby Fisher had made a name for herself, the award-winning Southern chef and businesswoman was bombarded with requests for her recipes. Abby was more than happy to share over three decades of cookery know-how with her fans. But because Abby was born enslaved and raised on a South Carolina plantation where literacy for slaves was considered a crime, she could neither read nor write.

Like all the obstacles Abby faced in her life, illiteracy wasn't going to stop her. And in 1881, she became the second Black woman in America to publish a cookbook. (Malinda Russell was the first.) Abby authored it rather ingeniously, via dictation to nine volunteers, all of whom subsequently had their names and addresses printed on the first page of her book. *What Mrs. Fisher Knows About Old Southern Cooking* was released by the Women's Co-operative Printing Office, then headquartered on San Francisco's Montgomery Street.

Remarkably, Abby's book begins with a "Preface and Apology":

> Not being able to read or write myself, and my husband also having been without the advantages of an education . . . caused me to doubt whether I would be able to present a work that would give perfect satisfaction . . . The book will be found a complete instructor, so that a child can understand it and learn the art of cooking.

The dictation, however, was not without its flaws. Some of those assisting Abby in writing and compiling her recipes either struggled with her Southern accent or simply had never heard of the dishes. (Eight of her assistants were from San Francisco; one was based in Oakland.) As such, there are a few quirks in the text that stand as proof of the difficulty of the task Abby and her transcribers faced. Succotash is referred to as "Circuit Hash." Jambalaya is called "Jumberlie." And mayonnaise is listed as "Milanese Sauce."

Abby Fisher was born in Orangeburg, South Carolina, in 1831, the daughter of an enslaved woman and a white plantation owner. On the 1880 census, she reported that her father hailed from France — typical for many landowners in South Carolina at the time. From the moment she was big enough to reach the stove, Abby worked in the plantation kitchen and became an expert in Southern cooking. She would go on to use those skills for the betterment of her family when they left the South — and slavery — behind.

It's unclear when she gained her freedom, but Abby met and married her husband, Alexander C. Fisher, in Mobile, Alabama, in the late 1850s, before the Civil War commenced. Like his wife, Alexander was born into slavery and raised on a plantation. And like her, he was mixed-race. They had four children in Mobile, and another during a brief stay in Missouri as they journeyed to California. No one knows for sure how the Fishers made it all the way to San Francisco, but the best guess is that they joined a wagon train. It was an affordable means of travel that tended to welcome cooks with open arms — even those with five children in tow.

By the time Abby's cookbook came out in 1881, her family had doubled in size. In her recipe, "Pap for Infant Diet" — a combination of flour boiled in a sealed jar, added to boiling milk with added sugar — she noted: "I have given birth to eleven children and raised them all, and nursed them with this diet. It is a Southern plantation preparation." She added: "When the child has diarrhea, boil a two-inch stick of cinnamon in the pap."

It's not the only occasion in *What Mrs. Fisher Knows About Old Southern Cooking* that the chef deviates from straightforward food recipes in order to share remedies to ease sickness. Her "Blackberry

Syrup — For Dysentery in Children" is listed as "an old Southern plantation remedy among colored people." These moments remain brief but enlightening snapshots of how enslaved people took care of their families with so few means at their disposal.

Though much of what Abby describes in her cookbook still sounds delicious to this day — especially her pie and preserve recipes — not all of it translates so well for today's audiences. For example, the recipes for terrapin soup ("always have the female terrapins and put them alive in boiling water") and calf's head soup ("when the tongue is tenderly boiled or done, take it out") are not for the faint of heart.

In her own time, though, Abby's recipes couldn't be beaten. She ran her own pickles and preserves company, and in 1879, the Sacramento State Fair awarded her their prestigious "Diploma." In 1880, she won two medals at the San Francisco Mechanics' Institute Fair, one for "Best Pickles and Sauces," the other for "Best Assortment of Jellies and Preserves."

The end of Abby Fisher's life remains a mystery, and her important work came extraordinarily close to being lost after the 1906 earthquake and fire decimated San Francisco. Only when a copy of her cookbook reemerged in 1984 at a Sotheby's auction were her talents rediscovered. It was soon reprinted and back in circulation.

Today, *What Mrs. Fisher Knows About Old Southern Cooking* stands as not just an important historical document, but a testament to Abby Fisher's will to thrive under difficult circumstances. That her recipes continue to live on 140 years after she wrote them speaks to her determination, her irrefutable talent, and the Bay Area communities that joined forces to amplify them.

Tien Fuh Wu

DURING AN 1894 RAID on a Chinatown gambling den, police officers were so shocked by the burns, cuts and bruises that covered Tien Fuh Wu's tiny body, they were said to have tears in their eyes as they carried her away from the property. The two missionaries leading the rescue worked out of the Occidental Board's Presbyterian Mission House, five blocks away on Sacramento Street. Tien would go on to spend most of her life there — first as a defiant child, and later as the tenacious rescuer of thousands of young women and girls just like her.

Tien had arrived in San Francisco two years earlier, after her father had sold her to pay off gambling debts. Somewhere between the ages of six and ten years old, Tien was escorted to a boat under the pretense of being sent to visit her grandmother. Her father locked her inside a cabin onboard with only a toothbrush and washcloth, told her to eat her supper, and left without saying goodbye. She never saw her family again, despite attempting to locate them decades later.

From her native province of Zehjiang, China, Tien was first taken a hundred miles north to Shanghai, then on to San Francisco via steamship. There, she was forced to work in a brothel, The Peking, as a "mui tsai." Though the phrase translates from Cantonese to "little sister," her role was that of a domestic slave. When the owner of the brothel fell into debt, Tien was sold to a gambling den on Jackson Street, where she was forced into rigorous work and physically abused by her new owner.

When the children sold into the Chinatown mui tsai system reached their teens, they typically transferred from a life of domestic slavery into one of forced sex work. At the turn of the century in San Francisco, this kind of trafficking was rampant, and largely ignored by city authorities. The only real challenge to the system came in the form of Christian missionaries, keen to free the imprisoned women from what they saw as a life of sin.

Fifteen months after Tien was rescued, 23-year-old Donaldina Cameron arrived at the Mission Home to teach the girls how to sew, and within two years she had become Superintendent. Initially the willful child and the strict teacher butted heads, but over time, they grew to form a relationship that more closely resembled that of mother and daughter.

With no ability to speak Chinese, Donaldina employed girls from the Mission House to act as her translators and aides. When Tien was in her teens, Donaldina's favorite aide, Leung Yuen Qui, contracted tuberculosis. Tien volunteered to nurse the gravely ill woman, and was witness to her death and the emotional devastation it caused Donaldina. She decided to step up to take Leung's place. It was the beginning of a working relationship that would last both of their lifetimes and save the lives of thousands of trafficked girls and women.

Earning $5 a month, Tien translated for Donaldina during court cases and helped supervise the Mission House. Most important of all, she accompanied Donaldina on dangerous rescues, some of which took many months and intense investigation to orchestrate.

Tien's role was of vital importance, not just due to her ability as a translator, but also because she put the rescued girls at ease. Many of them believed they would be in even greater danger if taken into the charge of white people. Tien — sometimes pointing to her own scars as evidence of her understanding — was the only one who could truly reassure them they were safe.

Tien's bravery cannot be overstated. Though everyone working at the Mission House received threats, Tien was targeted more than most because she herself was Chinese and therefore viewed as a traitor by the brothel owners in Chinatown. She was sent so many threats for doing rescue and interpretation work that, after each major rescue, Donaldina would routinely stop her 4'11" colleague from going out alone for weeks at a time.

Despite the danger, the Mission House had a tendency to emerge unscathed. Though the building had to be reconstructed, not only did the organization survive the 1906 earthquake, everyone living and working there also survived the flu epidemic of 1918 and 1919, despite most of the women in the home being struck down with the illness. Tien and the home's Assistant Superintendent, Ethel Higgins, are credited with nursing everyone back to health.

By the 1930s, as Donaldina readied herself for retirement, Tien took on even more responsibility, making public appearances to raise funds and awareness, while also dealing with the immigration woes of the women in their care. She also acted as a travel guardian for women who had testified against slave dealers and even vetted potential grooms for the girls. (They called her "Auntie Wu.") Tien herself turned down a multitude of suitors. "Men are very useful," she once said, "when it comes to moving furniture."

When Tien eventually retired in 1951, Donaldina offered her the cottage next door to her own in Palo Alto, and the two lived side by side until Donaldina's death in 1968. Tien is said to have been at her mentor's side, reading from a Bible until the very end. When Tien passed away seven years later, she was buried next to her friend in Donaldina's family plot at the Evergreen Cemetery in Los Angeles.

Her small headstone belies the huge importance of the life she lived. It reads only: "Tien Fuh Wu 1886–1975."

Mary Kelly

ON NOVEMBER 3, 1906, San Francisco residents, busy rebuilding the city after the April 18 earthquake and fire, were startled by a bizarre sight. It was a four-horse truck hauling a refugee "cottage" through the city streets, from Fillmore's Jefferson Square Park to Ingleside. Hanging out of one of the structure's windows was a woman clutching two placards. They read, "We demand a share of the Relief Fund," and "We demand a distribution of food and supplies."

The defiant protester was Mary Kelly, a cleaning woman whose family had been residing in a camp in Jefferson Square since they lost their home in the earthquake. After months of surviving in cold, leaky tents with her husband, Mary had begun squatting in the cottage — a small uninsulated shack with no sanitary provisions — out of desperation. After a month of Mary's refusal to move, heads of the city's Relief Corporation — the organization set up to distribute supplies and donations to refugees — ordered Mary's removal. As they hauled her away, she is said to have shouted, "I'll stay with this house if they take it to the end of the Earth!"

What was happening to Mary was an unusually harsh punishment doled out against an individual who had spent seven months persistently demanding dignity for those who had lost their homes in the disaster. In that time, Mary had transformed herself into one of the most tenacious activists in the city. Her efforts made her a leader in her community, but a sharp thorn in the side of city officials.

Once delivered to Ingleside, for three days, Mary stayed inside her cottage, which was still roped to the truck. She later reported that she was subjected to daily harassment from Relief Corporation employees who would "turn the crowd of thugs in a Tenderloin saloon, let alone a respectable woman."

On the third day, the Relief Corporation dismantled the cottage with Mary still inside. "There seemed about ten men with axes and crowbars and hatchets getting on the roof and ripping off the shingles," Mary later wrote in a pamphlet titled *Shame of the Relief.* This despite the fact that Mary was, according to the *San Francisco Call,* "worn and feeble" due to "a fast-developing case of grip or pneumonia sapping her energy."

So, what exactly had Mary done that spurred the Relief Corporation into taking such unusual action against her?

When city officials encouraged camp residents to leave the parks and find places to live, Mary was one of the loudest objectors. The rents in San Francisco were inflated after the fire, and many locals had lost their jobs. The working poor simply couldn't afford to move into new homes.

Soon, Mary was leading marches and making speeches on behalf of, in her words, a "steady, honest, hard-working class of people who never asked for charity from anyone and always paid their own way."

Mary didn't just go after the slow-moving bureaucracy that prevented the refugees from receiving their due, she went after the men at the head of the organizations. At one point, she accused "nearly every man that held any prominent position at the Relief Headquarters" of using relief money to buy expensive cars for their own personal use. At another, she led and made speeches in front of 3,000 protesters outside a banquet attended by city officials. "Let the whole world know," their banners read, "that while we are starving, they are feasting."

Of the attendees at that particular banquet, Mary later wrote, "Fearing that we might force an entrance and partake of their fine menu, they very quietly sneaked out of the back entrance of the hotel and rode away in their autos."

Mary's keen sense of injustice was not without cause. Financial assistance from the Relief Corporation, for example, was distributed on a tier system that benefited property owners, business owners and the well-connected first. The poorest, most hungry and least able to find work were often left to languish the longest.

One particularly egregious example of this occurred after the Relief Corporation attempted to sell some of the flour sent from Minneapolis to distribute to hungry refugees. When donors heard of the corporation's intent to sell, they objected. The corporation responded by dumping multiple barrels of the flour into the Bay. This prompted Mary, along with about a hundred other women, to storm the city's main relief warehouse on July 6, 1906, and walk out with 2,000 pounds of flour. "The women declared that the flour had been sent here for them," the *San Francisco Chronicle* reported, "and they were going to take it."

The war between Mary and city officials was granted a brief reprieve only after tragedy struck. In January 1907, two of Mary's daughters were murdered by their sister's husband. Joseph Rabley targeted the entire Kelly family after his wife, Mary Jr., left him after suffering beatings at home.

Just two months after they had paraded her through the streets, the Relief Corporation finally granted Mary a similar shelter at Dolores Park. The respite lasted a mere eight months. That August, the City ordered the refugees to relocate their cottages out of the park. Unable to come up with the money to do so, Mary and her husband stayed put as long as they could. On September 28, 1907, their cottage was torn down, leaving the couple to sleep entirely unsheltered.

It's unknown when exactly Mary's war with the city ceased. But her own ending was not an unhappy one. On October 18, 1911, the *Chronicle* reported that Mary was among the first wave of women who registered to vote in California. She listed her occupation as "a nurse and labor unionist."

She probably would have preferred the description the *Chronicle* once gave her, however: "The arch agitator of the refugees."

Clara Elizabeth Chan Lee

ON NOVEMBER 8, 1911, Clara Elizabeth Chan Lee put on her finest hat, went to the southeast corner of Lake Merritt, and entered the imposing facade of the Alameda County Courthouse. By her side was her husband Charles, her friend Emma Tom Leung and Emma's husband. Women had won voting rights in California just one month earlier, and now Clara and Emma were about to make history. They were the first Chinese-American women to register to vote in the United States.

After the registration papers were signed under the watchful eye of Assistant County Clerk W. B. Reith, Clara took little time to celebrate. Her work on behalf of Chinese-American women was only just beginning, and her community still had many metaphorical mountains to climb. Still, this was a historic first step — one that had seemed impossible just a few years earlier.

At the dawn of the 20th century, women of Asian descent living in California faced imposing barriers of both sexism and racism. The former was exacerbated by ongoing sex trafficking, which not only enslaved the women caught in that network, but also served to impose demeaning stereotypes on all Asian women. The latter was effectively codified by the highest echelons of the American government: The Page Act of 1875 prohibited Chinese women from immigrating to the United States; and the 1882 Chinese Exclusion Act blocked Chinese laborers from entering the country. These laws were still in effect — and would not be repealed for decades to come.

Less than two years after becoming the first Asian American woman to register to vote, Clara started the Chinese Women's Jeleab (Self-Reliance) Association. The organization saw education as key to acquiring freedom, independence and respect. Its incorporation papers, filed at the State Capitol, declared the group's purpose as "social intercourse, benevolent work, educational advantages, and mutual assistance and benefit."

The association distinguished itself by being staunchly independent, even avoiding any religious affiliation — deeply unusual for clubs of the era. Instead, it modeled itself after the Chinese Native Sons of the Golden State. (While the Native Sons organization prohibited female membership until 1973, it did make its Oakland headquarters available for the Jeleab Association to hold meetings.) Additionally, Clara's group was not shy about using newspapers to spread its message.

On September 22, 1913, the Jeleab Association published a manifesto of sorts in the Chinese newspaper *Chung Sai Yat Po*. "How can men . . . presume to be superior to women, trampling them underfoot, humiliating them, and making them serve men's every whim?" it queried. "Before one can be self-reliant, one must have education . . . If we women are to become independent, we must form a large group so that we can cull and share ideas and benefit from each other . . . Our goal is to cultivate self-reliance in each of us and furthermore, to promote and propagate this concept in China, so as to strip away the black curtain that has blocked women's view of the sky for thousands of years."

Education remained a core focus of the group for the entirety of its existence. It offered women classes in literacy, as well as lessons in American sewing patterns. On February 8, 1914, after membership had swelled to more than 200 women, *The San Francisco Examiner* declared the Jeleab Association "The Most Unique Club in America." The article gave prominent space to Clara as the association's founding president.

Despite its successes, the Chinese Women's Jeleab Association lasted only a few years. (Clara later noted that geographical challenges became an impediment to getting women together for meetings.) The group's decision to disband did nothing, however, to discourage the women's ongoing fight for education and independence. Most simply joined other clubs in its place. Clara herself joined the Chinese YWCA, established in 1916, as well as the Fidelis Coterie, a philanthropic Chinese women's club, and the International Institute.

Clara would spend the rest of her life assisting others, performing volunteer work to benefit both women and the Bay Area's Chinese community. And that was a lot of years of dedication — Clara Elizabeth Chan Lee died in 1993, at the age of 107. Her spirit endures in the generations of women who have continued her legacy: self-reliance over servitude.

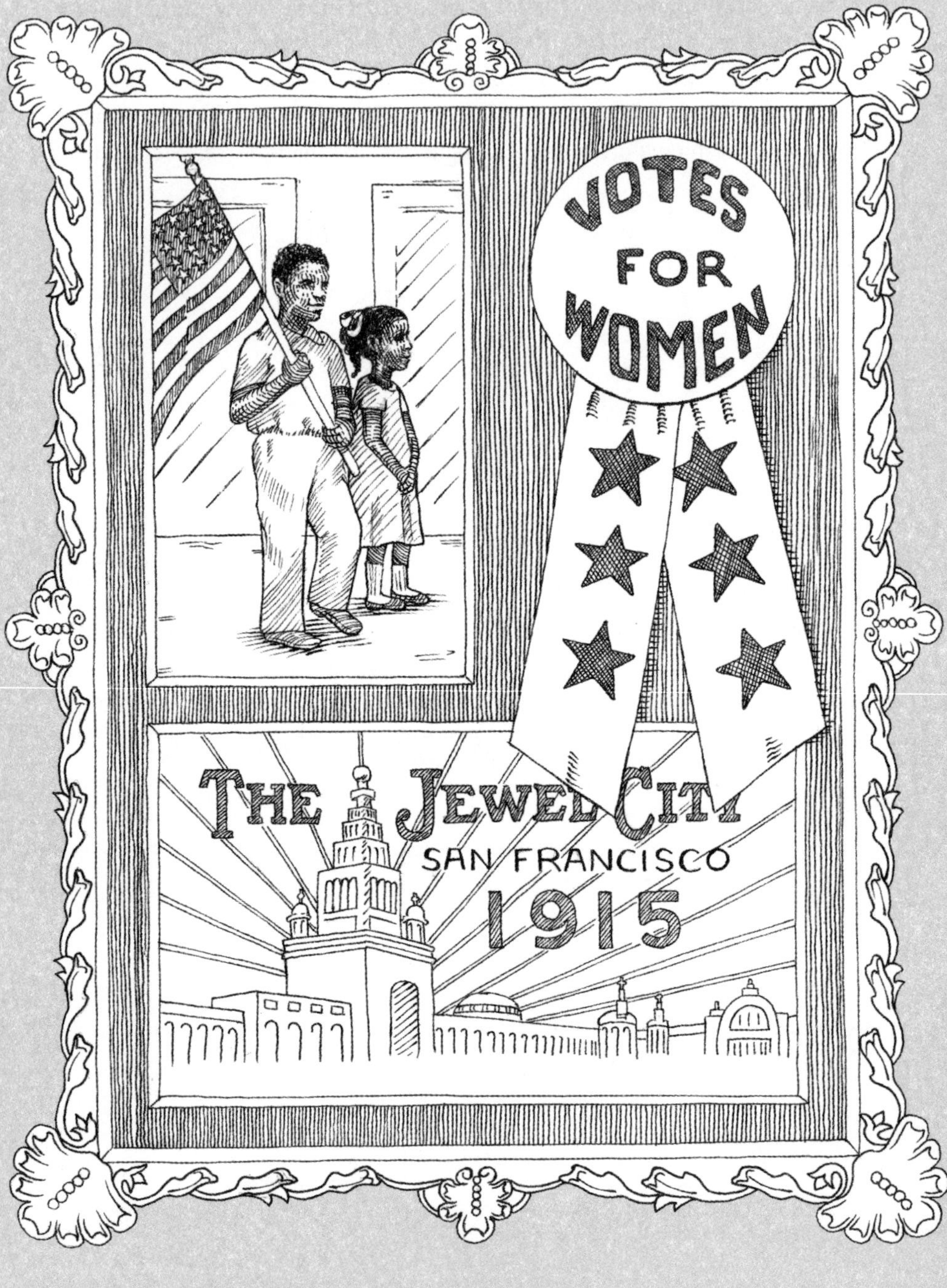
VOTES
FOR
WOMEN
THE JEWEL CITY
SAN FRANCISCO
1915

Myra Virginia Simmons

IN 1915, SAN FRANCISCO'S Panama-Pacific International Exposition heralded itself as a showcase of modernity and progress. But for the duration of its nearly yearlong run, the sprawling fair sold tickets to games and presentations so blatantly racist they sparked a Black-led demonstration that reverberated across the Bay area.

In the amusement section of the fair — known as the Joy Zone — booths like The African Dip, Soa Kum and Dixieland used enormous racist effigies on their exteriors to attract visitors. The Dixieland booth even peddled old lies about "the antebellum days in the South," when "the slaves were about the happiest and most carefree beings on earth." Nearby, in the Palace of Food Products, at the Sperry Flour Booth, Black women sold pancakes while dressed in full "mammy" attire.

After four months of witnessing these displays, Black communities from around the Bay Area converged on San Francisco's Ferry Building and formed a parade. The turnout was enormous; the *Oakland Sunshine* reported, "Everybody shut up shop and [got] themselves across the channel." A jubilant demonstration of flower-covered floats, choirs, flag-waving schoolchildren, streetcars full of Black women's clubs and everyday workers moved down Market Street and, at Van Ness, entered the Joy Zone. The parade then proudly marched across the entire fair.

This was Alameda County Day: an event intricately organized not just to dispel the stereotypes on show at the fair, but to illustrate Black people's contributions to the city, county and state. Leaving race out of the event's title was a very specific decision — organizers had scrapped plans for a "Negro Day" just months earlier. Participants had no interest in being tokenized. This wasn't merely about skin tone; it was a demand to be seen and treated as fellow, equal citizens.

At the time, the *San Francisco Chronicle* called the event "a revelation." Journalist Delilah L. Beasley wrote in the *Oakland Sunshine*: "The mere fact that colored children marched through the streets of San Francisco, carrying the Stars and Stripes, showed a decided advance and change of feeling toward the colored race in these parts."

The chairman of the committee that organized Alameda County Day wasn't a man at all. She was a 35-year-old Black woman by the name of Myra Virginia Simmons. Her day jobs might have been decidedly low-key — the Oakland resident sold newspapers and worked as a domestic cook. But, to women and people of color around the Bay Area, she was a formidable campaigner and community leader.

Myra had already served in an impressive number of capacities by the time Alameda County Day occurred on June 10, 1915. She was chair of the Women's Civic and Progressive League in Oakland; president of the Colored American Equal Suffrage League; a sometime speaker before the Woman's Christian Temperance Union; a leader of the Alameda County Colored Americans; and president of the Civic Center Auxiliary, a Black women's club.

Prior to Alameda County Day, the Civic Center Auxiliary had also taken the lead in a large protest against the conditions in San Quentin for inmates of color. Later it led protests alongside the NAACP against the glorification of the KKK and vilification of Black men in the 1916 movie *The Birth of a Nation.* But the majority of Myra's activist energy was spent on gaining voting rights for women.

After California women narrowly earned the right to vote in 1911 — by a margin of just 3,587 votes — Myra only worked harder. The November 23, 1911, edition of the *San Francisco Call* newspaper reported that she was actively educating women about their voting rights and encouraging them to be politically active. She even went on to serve as a precinct captain during the first California election open to women.

The national battle for women's suffrage, however, was still to be won, and women's clubs were of vital importance, both socially and politically, in achieving this. Black women's clubs, like Myra's Civic Center Auxiliary and Alameda County's Fannie Jackson Coppin Club, were focused on both civil and voting rights. Other women's clubs, like San Francisco's Votes for Women Club (led by the Pacific coast's first female lawyer, Clara Shortridge Foltz), were more singular in their focus.

The congressional passage of the 19th Amendment in 1919 was made possible by the dogged work of these women's organizational and outreach efforts. Myra herself was such an active campaigner that her name regularly showed up in newspapers around the Bay, as she led high-profile planning meetings with her peers. (On just one page of the March 29, 1915, issue of the *Oakland Sunshine*, she is mentioned in three separate stories.)

Many thousands of women fought for suffrage in the first decades of the 20th century, but Myra was a natural-born leader for whom no civic challenge was too great. She spent much of her later life in San Francisco, and lived to see the passage of 1964's Civil Rights Act. Myra Virginia Simmons died one year later at the age of 84.

Bertha Wright

IT ALL STARTED IN 1913, with a clinic housed inside an old donkey barn. The improvised medical practice was operated by a nurse so formidable and determined, not only did she provide all of the equipment needed to make the clinic functional, she worked without pay until it had sufficient donations to survive.

The nurse's name was Bertha Wright, and the clinic was all part of her larger mission to open a hospital dedicated to the care of babies and children in Oakland and Berkeley. Fifteen months after her practice in the barn opened its doors, Bertha's hard work paid off with the opening of the area's first children's hospital — an institution that started in an old mansion, but continues to survive to this day as UCSF's Benioff Children's Hospital. (It was renamed in 2014, after decades as Children's Hospital Oakland. In its earliest days, it was known simply as the Baby Hospital.)

Bertha's reputation as a dedicated and hardworking nurse was established far earlier than the hospital. Born in Piedmont, the middle child of three, she graduated from the California Women's Hospital School of Nursing in San Francisco in 1901, at the age of 25. She went on to work both there and at the Nurses' Settlement House in Potrero Hill, where she served a large population of struggling immigrants. After the 1906 earthquake and fires, Bertha tended to the sick and wounded in refugee camps all over the city.

In 1907, as the Bay Area struggled to rebuild, community groups and a variety of charities banded together to form the Charitable Organization Society of Berkeley. Wright was appointed Home Secretary and, while serving in that role, helped to establish the Berkeley Day Nursery, the first organization of its kind in California to offer subsidized childcare.

The nursery was funded by the City of Berkeley, the Berkeley Community Chest, the United Crusade, public donations and sliding-scale payments from parents. Prior to the nursery opening, working women were forced to leave their children at local orphan asylums while they did their jobs. The nursery continued caring for local children until 1965.

In 1910, Bertha also became the first district nurse to serve underprivileged children in Alameda County. In her mission to get care to the needy, she went on to co-found the Public Health Nurses' Association of Alameda County and also taught public health nursing at UC Berkeley. In her role as a visiting nurse, Bertha is said to have journeyed to hundreds of homes a week via her trusty horse and buggy. It was during these visits that Bertha became aware of the overwhelming need for hospital services that were dedicated specifically to the needs of children.

During one 1912 meeting of the Berkeley Commission of Public Charities, it was noted that:

> Ever since Miss Wright has been in Berkeley, she has [believed] that much of her effort has been wasted because of this lack of a proper place for sick children. The need of a hospital for the babies among whom we work is especially urgent because of the crowded home conditions, a certain ignorance on the part of the parents and their limited incomes, reasons which do not exist in the homes of those in more comfortable circumstances.

Wright was determined that children should not suffer due to the financial hardships of their parents. When the Baby Hospital first opened on September 16, 1914, the cost was supposed to be $1 a day for ward beds and $2.50 for private rooms, but fewer than 10 percent of patients usually paid the full fee — if any fee at all. The hospital was able to stay open only because of a tireless group of local women who relentlessly fundraised at fairs, dinners and fashion shows, and in their own communities.

At the time of its opening, the hospital housed a 20-bed ward on the first floor, a 10-bed ward on the second, and five private rooms. The staff was small: three nurses, a secretary, a cook and a houseboy. Doctors were summoned from other hospitals when their assistance was required. During that first year, the Baby Hospital treated 611 children. That same year, Bertha's smaller clinic on the property saw more than 6,000 patients. In 1916, the hospital established a dental clinic. A maternity clinic on the property helped to safely deliver newborns.

Even before the hospital was officially opened, Bertha had begun holding prenatal and baby hygiene classes at her clinic. She also helped organize the first "baby saving fairs" on the West Coast. But Bertha's dedication to children was not limited to her working life.

During her time with the Charitable Organization Society, she had met social worker Mabel Weed, who then played a key role in fundraising for the Baby Hospital. The women moved in together in the early 1920s and went on to raise three adopted children, Philip, Barbara and Jean. They also fostered a great many others. In fact, the 1940 census shows that, when Bertha was 62 and Mabel was 68, they were still fostering children in Palo Alto. Bertha continued to do so on her own after Mabel's death in 1957.

Bertha Wright was blessed with an uncommon drive and took an unconventional approach to life. She is also said to have been rather imposing. Murray Morgan's book *The Hospital Women Built for Children* describes Wright: "Tall and rawboned, dedicated and un-demure, she could face down a practical objection with a skeptical glance."

Bertha passed away in 1971 just one month shy of her 95th birthday, after a lifetime spent in the service of children, women and those living on the margins. She was buried close to her beloved Mabel in Alto Mesa Cemetery, Palo Alto.

Elizabeth Ashe

ON AUGUST 16, 1917, Elizabeth Ashe found herself in Northern France, close to the front lines of World War I, in the middle of an air raid.

"The Tocsin [siren] sounded and the fearsome took to the cellar," the nurse wrote in a letter three days later. "I figured it is as dangerous as crossing Market Street . . . "

The casual bravery exhibited in that letter was present throughout Elizabeth's life. Whether taking care of the neediest communities in San Francisco or helping impoverished new mothers and soldiers in France, Elizabeth's life was spent in enthusiastic service of others. So enthusiastic, in fact, she spent three years persuading the Red Cross to send her to France in the first place. The organization had been hesitant to send a woman in her mid-40s to serve in a war zone.

Born in 1869, Elizabeth became a community activist in her teens while teaching Sunday School at the chapel that would later become Grace Cathedral. During her classes, she got to know her neighbors from Telegraph Hill — mostly immigrants who often lived in unsanitary conditions without heat or plumbing. Elizabeth, born into privilege, found herself deeply concerned, particularly when it came to the number of unsupervised children she encountered.

When epidemics of diphtheria, tuberculosis and typhoid broke out, Elizabeth wasn't discouraged from working in the area. Instead, she and her friend Alice Griffith established the city's first settlement house — an organization designed to assist struggling families with healthcare, daycare and education. Elizabeth was just 21 at the time. Today, the house lives on as the Telegraph Hill Neighborhood Center.

In 1911, Elizabeth and Alice also opened the Arequipa Sanitarium for tuberculosis patients in Marin County. For decades, Arequipa had a long waiting list for admission, due in part to its state-of-the-art facilities and low cost for patients. The clinic was also a leader in occupational therapy, establishing a pottery program that went on to achieve world renown.

Elizabeth's bold approach to life was, in many ways, influenced by the work she did helping San Francisco residents recover from the 1906 earthquake. Coming shortly after her graduation from nursing school, the work left such a grim impression on her that everything Elizabeth did afterward seemed somehow manageable by comparison.

In Elizabeth's fascinating collection of wartime correspondence, *Intimate Letters from France*, one of her letters to Alice from "Somewhere in France," states:

> No other women have ever been so near the lines . . . Christ on his crucifix in many villages is the only thing erect, where women and little children by thousands must work in the fields under shell fire wearing gas masks . . . [It] did not make the dreadful impression on me I anticipated, it is not a circumstance to our fire.

During her time in France, Elizabeth tackled the country's high infant mortality rate by educating new mothers. From Paris tenements to country farms, Elizabeth taught new parents the best ways to care for babies, including prenatal hygiene, healthy feeding and infection avoidance. She even helped establish a clinic in Paris, advised those working in "orphan asylums" and still somehow found the time to teach French children how to play leapfrog.

Remarkably, Elizabeth spent her days off during that time tending to injured soldiers at Neuilly's American Military Hospital, writing home of the hellish conditions:

> The wounded continue to pour in night and day, it is impossible to handle them properly. I am duty in

> the receiving ward (a big garage which holds about 100 stretchers, packed so closely together you can't step between.)

The purpose of releasing her letters as a book was so that Elizabeth might raise funds for causes close to her heart. But the collection also gave readers a vivid view of the horrors of war. The *San Francisco Chronicle* declared the book "not only informative, but essentially human. One sees the routine life of the nurse both in base hospitals and nearer the firing line . . . Brave girl."

On her return to San Francisco in July 1919, Elizabeth went back to work at Hill Farm in Marin County — also known as the Bothin Convalescent Home for women and children — which she had helped to establish in 1910 with the help of steel magnate Henry E. Bothin. She also acted as director of Public Health Nurses for the American Red Cross and publicly campaigned to establish health centers in every community.

Elizabeth Ashe died in 1954, but her legacy of community service remains scattered across San Francisco and the North Bay, with the continued existence of organizations she worked tirelessly to establish.

Alma de Bretteville Spreckels

SHE WAS A DANISH IMMIGRANT who grew up on the rough side of town. She was a scandalous nude model with a reputation. She enjoyed skinny-dipping well into old age. And if it wasn't for this controversial livewire, San Francisco would have neither the Legion of Honor nor the Maritime Museum.

Her name was Alma de Bretteville Spreckels, but her more fitting nickname was "Big Alma" — a moniker that captured not only her 6-foot-tall stature, but her outgoing, devil-may-care personality too.

Alma's greatest gifts to the city all happened after her 1908 marriage to Adolph Bernard Spreckels, the wealthy and successful son of sugar refinery entrepreneur Claus Spreckels. But Alma was already a local celebrity in her own right by the time she met him in 1902.

Adolph first fell in love with Alma after she was hired by sculptor Robert Ingersoll Aitken to pose as the Goddess of Victory for Union Square's Dewey Monument. Despite his being 24 years her senior, Adolph and Alma were a good match. Adolph had some of the same anarchic impulses that drove Alma. He famously shot *San Francisco Chronicle* editor Michael de Young in 1884, after the paper printed a series of unflattering articles about his father. (Adolph was acquitted after he pleaded insanity and self-defense.) Even more significantly, Adolph shared Alma's generous spirit. He was a man who had persuaded his father to contribute to the construction of Golden Gate Park's band shell, as well the building of the Dewey Monument. She was a woman who responded to the 1906 earthquake by organizing community kitchens.

After they finally tied the knot, Alma and Adolph's honeymoon involved a trip around the world. Still, Alma took nothing for granted. Legend has it, she coined the term "sugar daddy" to affectionately describe her husband's generosity. The phrase's longevity is fitting. There was nothing temporary about Adolph's desire to give Alma whatever she wanted. Because of him, Alma finally had access to the wealth that she had been striving for her whole life.

Born in 1881, Alma was raised with four brothers and one sister in San Francisco's Sunset District, back when it was still known as the "Outside Lands." To make ends meet, Alma's mom, Mathilde, transformed the front room of their home into a Danish bakery. Alma's brothers' bedroom was sometimes used as a massage studio. Mathilde even laundered other people's clothes in a Cow Hollow lagoon to make extra money. Alma was forced out of school and into work in her early teens, but naturally followed her mother's industrious example. Alma delivered laundry to the mansions in town. She worked as a stenographer. Her nude modeling later came about because it was the quickest way for her to make good money.

After marriage to Adolph, Alma had three children in four years — though she made for a reluctant mother. To accommodate their growing family, in 1913 Adolph finished building Alma her dream mansion at 2080 Washington Street, opposite Lafayette Park. Lavish parties became regular occurrences, though San Francisco's social elites shunned Alma relentlessly. Instead, she happily hosted fascinating guests including author Jack London, Folies Bergère dancer Loie Fuller, and even the Prince and Princess of Siam.

Alma was much more than a mere party girl, though. During both world wars, when Alma wasn't holding high-profile charity auctions, fairs and raffles at venues like San Francisco's Palace Hotel, she did so out of her own home. Alma tirelessly raised money for causes close to her heart: aid for Romania, post-war house-building in France, a milk fund for Belgian orphans. She sent medical supplies and musical instruments to troops overseas.

During the Second World War, she sent a washing machine to a Navy station when she found out cooks were having to handwash their clothes.

Her wartime charitable organization, the League for Servicemen, opened a recreation center for troops. Alma also saw to it that thousands of radios, toiletries, typewriters and athletic supplies were sent to those serving overseas. One Navy commander credited Alma with saving the lives of at least 250 men via her swift delivery of much-needed medical equipment.

Alma's greatest legacy lies at San Francisco's Legion of Honor, however. Inspired by the Palais de la Légion d'Honneur in Alma's beloved Paris, the museum cost Adolph over a million dollars to build. After much campaigning, Alma managed to acquire donations of art from Belgium, Romania, Serbia, Poland and France. Sadly, by the time the museum opened, Alma was in mourning. Adolph had died mere months before the Legion's doors opened.

The loss hit Alma hard, but it didn't stop her from forging ahead with big ideas. In the late 1930s, Alma became obsessed with the idea of creating a maritime museum for San Francisco. It was a thought that had been brewing in her mind for some time. Speaking to the San Francisco Beautiful Committee in 1937, Alma expressed her desire to see more "centers to house not only maritime collections, but mining, industrial exhibits and other typically California displays in which visitors to the city would be interested." Alma became a trustee for the new maritime museum, was instrumental in raising money for its founding, and donated important collections to fill its walls.

The end of Alma's life was significantly quieter than the beginning. After her son died during a bar altercation in 1961, she stopped socializing and retreated to the comforts of her mansion. Alma died in 1968 at the age of 87, and her funeral, described by the *Examiner* as "perhaps the most opulent in the city's history," was held at her beloved Legion of Honor.

After her death, paying tribute to Big Alma, one newspaper called her "the grandest of grande dames — a lady who not only gave generously, but lived in high old style, paddling around in her Roman pool daily, nipping appreciatively at her pitcher of martinis, and always talking straight and dry. . . . A San Franciscan, true and through."

Delilah L. Beasley

IN 1923, THE *OAKLAND TRIBUNE* started a groundbreaking new weekly column. "Activities Among Negroes" was authored by Delilah L. Beasley. In her writing, Delilah not only bucked racist stereotypes by putting an emphasis on achievements in the Black community, but also managed to shine a light on the barriers that people of color, and women, faced in their everyday lives.

Even when she was writing about local issues, Delilah's vision was big picture. She had an instinct and understanding that her column had the potential to act as a direct line to both the white establishment, which could effect legal change, and the average white household, which might encourage a social one. Beasley's journalistic ambitions started when she was still in her teens and, from the beginning, crossed racial lines. Her earliest work was printed by the African American newspaper *Cleveland Gazette* and the mainstream white publication, *Cincinnati Enquirer.*

Born on September 9 in either 1867 or 1871, Delilah had writing ambitions that were temporarily halted in her teens after both of her parents died. After she and her four siblings were separated, Delilah was forced to drop out of school and become a maid for a judge in Cincinnati.

Determined to improve her position in life, Delilah studied hydrotherapy, medical gymnastics and other elements of anatomy until she was able to become a massage therapist. Over the years, Delilah worked in sanitariums and resorts in Illinois, New York and Michigan. For a time, Delilah was known for easing the physical woes of pregnant women with head massage. She eventually found herself in Northern California in 1910, after becoming a full-time nurse for one of her clients who had moved to Berkeley.

In California, Delilah began writing once more, delicately straddling racial divisions in the press. After writing an article about the pro-KKK film *Birth of a Nation* for the *Oakland Tribune* in 1915, Delilah was forced to follow it up with a piece in the *Oakland Sunshine* defending her decision to do so. "News of special interest to us as a people ought to be discussed in our own papers among ourselves," she wrote. "But, if a bit of news would have a tendency to better our position in the community, then it should not only be published in our own race papers, but in the papers of the other race as well."

In 1919, Delilah self-published her book *The Negro Trail-Blazers of California*, which she had painstakingly researched over the course of eight years, inspired by history classes she took at U.C. Berkeley. Publishing the book herself was a financial risk that put her in debt for several years, but one that paid off in a larger sense, giving a voice to the Black pioneers who had largely been written out of history. In the foreword to the book, the managing editor of the *California Eagle* wrote:

> In gathering the data for this most unique volume, she has sacrificed money, and health. She, however, shall feel well repaid for her labor if, through the perusal of these pages, there shall be an incentive to even greater efforts by the Negro Race in this State in the future.

This wasn't the only time Delilah made financial sacrifices to follow her calling — she earned far less writing for the *Oakland Tribune* than she would have made working full-time as a massage therapist.

After her profile was raised across the Bay Area, thanks in large part to her *Tribune* column, Delilah began to travel around the country in the hopes of persuading the editors of major newspapers everywhere to stop using racist language in print. She also regularly spoke at rallies and protests. So determined was Delilah to advance the rights of African

Americans and women, she joined just about every civic club she could find. These included the NAACP, the National Association of Colored Women, the Linden Center Young Women's Christian Association, the Alameda County League of Colored Women Voters and the Oakland Council of Church Women.

A group of young Black women in the East Bay were so inspired by Delilah's commitment to these groups, they formed one of their own, named after her. Rodger Streitmatter's 1994 book *Raising Her Voice: African-American Women Journalists Who Changed History* notes that: "Members defined their purpose by choosing a word to correspond to each letter in the name D-E-L-I-L-A-H L. B-E-A-S-L-E-Y: Deeds Ever Lasting In Lending A Hand. Let's Be Ever Alert Serving Lovingly Every Year."

Delilah's simultaneous activism and work as a reporter sometimes meant that she found herself having to report on her own achievements. On such occasions, her humility shone through her text. "There was introduced Friday January 27 in the California Legislature an Anti-Lynching Bill at the request of this writer," she wrote in 1933. "This writer knowing that the editors of *The Oakland Tribune* have for 20 years fought lynching through some editorials, decided to ask Assemblyman Wm. Knewland, assistant publisher of *The Tribune* to jointly introduce the bill with Assemblyman Frederick Madison Roberts of Los Angeles. . . . Many women's organizations endorsed the intentions of this writer to have this bill introduced."

Delilah continued writing her column for the *Tribune* until her death in 1934. Her tombstone in the Y section of St. Mary's Cemetery in Oakland offers simply her name and dates. Delilah's own words might have proved a more fitting tribute to her tenacity.

"Every life casts its shadow," she once wrote. "My life plus others make a peer to move the world. I, therefore, pledge my life to the living world of brotherhood and mutual understanding between the races."

Louise Arner Boyd

BEING BORN INTO PRIVILEGE does not always guarantee a life of ease and comfort. Louise Arner Boyd's life stands as a clear example. Born in San Rafael in 1887, Louise enjoyed an idyllic childhood bouncing between San Rafael and a lavish family farm in Danville with her two brothers and well-to-do parents. That was until the age of 13, when her big brother Seth suddenly died. Just eight months later, her other brother Jack followed, both victims of heart conditions. While Louise's mother, Louise Cook Arner, held herself together with a stiff upper lip, Louise's father, John Franklin Boyd, collapsed into grief at losing his heirs. Then in 1919, tragedy struck again. John died after a fall down the stairs just six months after his wife had died of an illness.

Louise, at the age of 32, was left entirely alone, an heiress to a fortune that she had no idea what to do with. It would take five years, a couple of cross-country outings, and two long trips to Europe for Louise to figure that out.

By 1924, Louise realized she was in possession of an unquenchable thirst for adventure. After two years of planning, she embarked on an expedition from Norway to Franz Josef Land, an archipelago in the Arctic Ocean that had been recently seized by Russia. The islands were notoriously treacherous to reach, and the expedition was the first of its kind, planned by, financed by, and inclusive of a woman. The journey would take six weeks, with an onboard meteorologist collecting data while Louise acted as photographer. By the end, she had captured 700 images and shot 25,000 feet of film, most of which she later donated to the American Geographical Society.

Her epic six weeks in the Arctic didn't quell Louise's passion for adventure, even when other missions made it abundantly clear that these kinds of outings were extraordinarily risky. In 1928, an Italian aeronautical engineer by the name of Umberto Nobile went missing on his way back from the North Pole. In response, a Norwegian explorer named Roald Amundsen went in search of Nobile — and also promptly went missing. Louise responded to this by running in the direction of the danger and searching 10,000 miles of Arctic Ocean for the men. Nobile eventually emerged of his own accord, while Amundsen perished. Regardless, Louise was awarded the prestigious Norwegian Chevalier Cross of the Order of Saint Olav for her fearless efforts. One rescue coordinator told Louise in writing, "You volunteered for the hardest and most dangerous cruises, showing devotion and courage."

Unperturbed by the loss of Amundsen's entire crew, Louise continued to make regular expeditions to the most inhospitable places on Earth. In 1931, she went to Greenland and documented a glacier and a previously unknown land mass. She returned in 1933 with a geologist, botanist, surveyor and physiographer. She embarked on further explorations in 1937 and 1938. Louise photographed the frigid environs thoroughly, documenting her work in several books including *The Fiord Region of East East Greenland* (1935) and *Polish Countrysides* (1937). One review of the latter stated: "Miss Boyd is not only to be congratulated on the work of her camera, but must be warmly thanked for compiling a permanent record of so many of the distinctive features of a country where changes are taking place rapidly from day to day."

Louise's work remains vitally important for this very reason. Her photos and records continue to provide a baseline for climate change investigations today.

In 1941, Louise faced one of her biggest challenges yet, studying the effects of polar magnetism on radio communications in Greenland, in association with the National Bureau of Standards (today's National Institute of Standards and Technology). Her work there was so impressive, she was transferred to the War Department as an expert consultant. She worked for military intelligence between 1942 and 1944.

Louise still wasn't done. A decade after the end of World War II, just when it seemed like she was settling into a more comfortable role as the Most Interesting Dinner Guest in San Francisco, Louise decided to become the first woman to ever fly over the North Pole — at the age of 67, no less. She completed the 16-hour non-stop flight with aplomb. She later reminisced about her moment of glory:

> Directly below us, 9,000 feet down, lay the North Pole! No cloud in the brilliant blue sky hid our view of this glorious field of shining ice. . . . In a moment of reverent awe the crew and I gave thanks for this priceless sight. We crossed the Pole, then circled it, flying "around the world" in a matter of minutes. Then we departed. My Arctic dream had come true.

All told, "the Ice Queen," as she was dubbed, was so globally respected for her exploratory work, data gathering and analysis that Louise received a variety of honors and awards from Denmark, Sweden, France and Italy. She also had part of Greenland named after her. "Louise Boyd Land" sits at an elevation of 6,535 feet. In 1960, she was given the honor of becoming the first female councilor of the American Geographic Society.

Louise died in San Francisco two days before her 85th birthday. Rather than be buried with the rest of her family in their crypt at Mount Tamalpais Cemetery, she opted to have her ashes scattered into the Arctic Ocean. Throughout her life, she was a special combination of smart, fearless and hardy, and no matter how long she spent out in freezing waters, she held true to her own sense of decorum:

"I like the pleasant things most women enjoy," she once noted, "even if I do wear breeches and boots on an expedition — even sleep in them at times. But I powder my nose before going on deck, no matter how rough the sea is."

Vivian Osborne Marsh

AFTER GRADUATING FROM HIGH SCHOOL in 1914, Vivian Osborne applied to study anthropology at U.C. Berkeley. A gifted student, she had earned outstanding grades at both Berkeley High and, prior to that, Houston High School.

But it wasn't enough.

At the time, U.C. Berkeley refused to admit any student who had been schooled even partially in Southern states unless that student also passed four additional entrance exams. Osborne completed only two — she was excused from the rest because her results on the first two were so exceptional that her example prompted the university to permanently scrap its discriminatory policies against students from the South.

That was just the first time that Vivian would transform U.C. Berkeley for the better. Not only was she the first Black woman to ever major in anthropology, she was also one of the first women to earn a master's degree there.

It was while working toward her master's degree that Vivian founded the university's first Black sorority, Delta Sigma Theta, and acted as its first president. By that time, having been a member of the Phillis Wheatley Club (part of the California State Association for Colored Women) for years, she understood well the power gained from working in organized groups.

After she graduated in 1922, Vivian embraced a life of activism, public service and leadership full-time. She and her new husband, Leon F. Marsh, lived in Berkeley, and their home on Grant Street quickly became a crucial hub for community organizers and political groups.

In 1928, Vivian became director of the Oakland junior branch of the NAACP — she would work alongside the anti-racist organization in one way or another for the rest of her life. And in 1929, Vivian established the Omega Sigma Alumnae Chapter so that U.C. Berkeley women could continue their involvement in Delta Sigma Theta after they'd graduated. She was Omega Sigma's first president, and in fact, her work for the sorority never ceased. In 1948, she and her sister Bessie founded the Patroness Club — a group of women who acted as mother figures to female sorority pledges who were far from home.

In 1931, while serving as secretary for the Northern Board of the California Federation of Colored Women's Clubs, Vivian fought hard to stop a racist bill that would have segregated children in recreational areas. The proposed law was written in response to a battle in Los Angeles to integrate public pools. Letters co-written by Vivian were reproduced in full in the *Oakland Tribune* as part of Delilah Beasley's "Activities Among Negroes" column.

The legislation was defeated.

Later in the decade, Vivian campaigned relentlessly at universities and women's clubs to help get anti-lynching legislation passed. In 1938, the *California Eagle* newspaper reported on a lecture-reception Vivian was hosting: "Her appearance in Los Angeles is expected to draw throngs and ovations similar to that received in the South," it wrote, "especially at Fisk University where [writer and civil rights activist] James Weldon Johnson gave up his scheduled appearance in order that students might hear her."

The anti-lynching bill ultimately failed to pass after four senators from Texas, Georgia and Florida filibustered for 30 days straight to block it. But the frustrating failure did nothing to dull Vivian's fighting spirit.

Throughout the 1930s, Vivian was focused on helping young Black people across the nation. As part of her role as Delta Sigma Theta's national president, she organized a traveling library for children in rural Georgia. Then she created a program called "Teen Lift," which covered travel and ticket costs for underprivileged Black children to attend operas, symphonies, concerts and other live events.

During the Great Depression, Vivian was the first Black woman on the West Coast to take on the position of state supervisor of the National Youth Organization (NYO). Working in the Division of Negro Affairs, she was tasked with finding jobs for unemployed people of color between the ages of 16 and 25 and ensuring that other parts of the organization were free from discriminatory practices. At one stage, Vivian wrote to every chamber of commerce across California and requested assistance in finding NYO workers positions in the private sector. Her idea was greeted with flagrantly racist response letters. She later noted, "The writers do not know they are writing to a Negro."

The advent of World War II did nothing to slow Vivian down. She took it upon herself to be a unit commander of the Women's Ambulance and Defense Corps of America. The women were trained in first aid, ambulance driving, nursing, rescue work, radio operations and infantry drills. They also sold war bonds and visited veterans in the hospital. By 1944, Vivian was so revered, she was invited to christen a Navy cargo ship (the *SS Ocean Telegraph*) in Oakland before it took its maiden voyage. She was elected vice president of the National Council of Negro Women in 1945, and quickly formed smaller councils in Oakland, Richmond, Fresno and Sacramento to aid in the organization's civil rights work.

In the 1950s, Vivian tackled social issues on both the political and personal fronts. An active member of the Republican Party, she sat on the Alameda County Republican Central Committee and the State Republican Legislative Council. She was also known to offer advice on racial issues to Democrats, and later in the decade, Berkeley's city council appointed her to their Planning Commission.

At the same time, Vivian worked with her husband to establish fraternal organizations, which provided scholarship grants to students and donations of money, food and clothing to members of the community in need.

Vivian suffered a stroke in 1986 while at a convention, and passed away soon after at the age of 88. Fortunately, five years earlier, the city of Berkeley had declared February 21 Vivian Osborne Marsh Day — a small token of gratitude for a life spent in tireless community service.

Mary Mammon

IN THE 1930S, young Asian American women in San Francisco didn't have a lot of job prospects. At home, these women often faced limiting cultural expectations. And in the wider world, discrimination was rife. Secretarial and administrative positions were off-limits, and even the most beautiful and talented girls couldn't find regular work as models or actors. For those unwilling to rush into marriage or perform manual labor, employment options were few and far between.

When Prohibition ended in 1933, however, opportunities arose. For those brave enough to embrace the thrills and spills of city nightlife, the new nightclubs opening up in Chinatown offered jobs. Bold young Asian American women became singers, dancers and showgirls, and entertained packed rooms of diverse audiences. One of these women was Mary Mammon.

For the first 16 years of her life, Mary lived in Clifton, Arizona. When her grandmother got sick, her mom — originally from San Francisco — moved Mary and her five older siblings to the city by the Bay. Mary was immediately struck by how segregated it was.

"At one time," she told Arthur Dong in an interview for his book *Forbidden City USA*, "the boundary line was Broadway. The Italians didn't cross over to the Chinese side and the Chinese didn't cross over to that side without causing some sort of fracas . . . the parks had signs that said 'No Chinese or dogs allowed.'"

In 1936 Mary tried her hand as a cocktail waitress at the Chinese Pagoda, situated at 830 Grant Avenue. A popular trend at the time was to have singing wait staff, and Mary jumped at the chance to perform for an audience. One of her most popular numbers was "A-Tisket-A-Tasket," the jazz standard popularized by Ella Fitzgerald. Meanwhile, she reached out to chorus lines across San Francisco and was turned down by all of them. "They didn't think a Chinese could do it," she told the *Sydney Morning Herald* in 1992. "Most people thought that Blacks had a lot of rhythm and Orientals had none."

In December of 1938, Mary was finally given the chance to expand her skills when the first Chinese nightclub in America opened at 363 Sutter Street. Forbidden City was the brainchild of Charlie Low, a bar owner originally from Nevada, and Mary was welcomed with open arms — she was one of the few chorus girls there with any experience at all.

"I shared the tastes of middle America," Mary said in 1992. "The nightclubs were not a cultural shock to me. They were quite nice. The days of the speakeasy were gone. I mainly remember that we had a lot of fun at Charlie Low's club, doing what we wanted to do. People were curious about us."

The club limped through its first year, struggling to find its tone and audience. But once it did, it inspired a rash of copycats in Chinatown. The Chinese Skyroom, Club Shanghai, Kubla Khan and Lion's Den all swiftly followed, offering the same joyful blend of Asian and American cultures. But the change in the neighborhood was not welcomed by everyone — and the female performers were judged most harshly of all.

"The Chinese families in San Francisco looked down on such things," Mary explained in *Forbidden City USA*. "Show your legs out there for people to see? It was unheard-of! Girls were taught to grow up and keep house, and we were supposed to get married at a certain time, and we were supposed to know how to take care of a house, and take of the children, and take care of your husband. This was just not part of the Chinese culture."

By the 1940s, Mary and her cohort at Forbidden City were a nationwide sensation. *Life* magazine had already brought national attention to the club in 1938 with an article about how it filled "a local cultural need," but it was during World War II when word really began to spread, thanks to the servicemen who visited while on leave. Once the military came, the press was quick to follow.

One newsreel of the time introduced the chorus girls in a beach setting. Wearing traditional Chinese dresses, the women begin the segment with what the newscaster describes as an "age-old dance" in order to "welcome Springtime." After a few moments, the seemingly demure women run behind a screen, fling off their clothes and emerge gleefully in modern swimsuits for a dance routine on the sand.

In June 1941, a syndicated Associated Press article presented a day in the life of Mary Mammon. Chinatown, it said, "once was reputed to hold all the sins and exotic charms of Old China, but a new generation, modern and American, has sprung up." After a series of photos of Mary performing, shopping, eating, studying, sunbathing, and walking through Chinatown in fashionable garb, the story concluded with a salient point. "Tourists may mourn the passing of the old Chinatown customs and fixtures, but for Mary and girls like her it has meant emancipation."

With the 1950s came a cultural shift that left Forbidden City and other nightclubs like it looking increasingly dated. Charlie Low finally sold the club in 1962. By that time, Mary was a single mom of two sons, having married in 1947 and divorced in 1955. When the club closed, she hung up her dancing shoes and took a job at Safeway. Mary never lost her love of music, though. In retirement, she sang in choirs and danced at the Berkeley Chinese Senior Center, where she was an active volunteer.

Mary Mammon died in 2002 at the age of 84, a beloved great-grandmother who never forgot her nightclub days. Her determination to live life on her own terms was an inspiration to other women, and it transformed the way white America saw a new generation of Asian Americans.

Enriqueta Andazola

WHEN HER FOUR SONS LEFT Sacramento to fight in World War II, Enriqueta Andazola's trepidation about what they might face was outshined by a stronger emotion: pride. Enriqueta — like other mothers of the half million Mexican Americans who fought in the war — was immensely proud of her boys for serving their country.

World War II was a watershed moment for members of America's Mexican and Latin American communities who had endured years of discrimination, segregation and poor housing conditions. After their years of active duty, returning soldiers started making demands for long-overdue civil rights and respect. It must have been heartening, then, for the veterans to find that some of the groundwork for this new battle had already been laid by the women they'd left at home. One of the most impactful of them was Enriqueta.

Born in Chihuahua, Mexico, in 1892, Enriqueta came to Sacramento in 1917 to escape the chaos and violence of the Mexican Revolution. Although she had worked as a schoolteacher in Chihuahua, she was now locked out of the profession of her choice, and her first job in California was at the Sacramento Wool Company. Enriqueta subsequently spent decades working at the Del Monte cannery.

Cannery work was the primary source of income for much of Sacramento's Chicana community at the time, and Enriqueta found a silver lining in the camaraderie and friendships she developed through the workplace. After her divorce, the cannery gave her a steady income on which to raise her sons, Joe (née José), Edgardo, John and Paul.

Though Enriqueta considered herself a proud American, it was never at the expense of her own cultural identity. As her granddaughter Diana Salgado Zuñiga would later note, "If there was anything she passed on to me, it was a true feeling of pride in being a Mexican. She assimilated into the society, but she kept her sense of culture."

Throughout her life, Enriqueta worked to keep Mexican traditions alive in Sacramento. She was instrumental in organizing and promoting Cinco de Mayo and Mexican Independence Day celebrations, and she was active in establishing community groups for Mexican Americans. These included a branch of Alianza Hispanoamericana — a community organization that educated, empowered and advocated for people of Mexican descent living in the United States.

Enriqueta's primary focus, though, was on establishing spaces by and for women. "Men had clubs," she once noted. "I felt that women deserved [clubs] too." So, in 1920, she founded Las Amigas Del Hogar (Friends of Homemakers), a women's group specifically for Chicanas. Nineteen years later, she established the Unión Femenil (Feminine Union). And in 1942, she co-founded Las Madres Mexicanas de Guerra (Mexican War Mothers), alongside her dear friend Antima Perez.

Though all women of the era were expected to join in the war effort, Las Madres went above and beyond. They tended to wounded soldiers in local military hospitals. They launched letter-writing campaigns and sent care packages to the soldiers abroad. They held dinners and dances to raise money for the Veterans Affiliated Council. They regularly donated money to Yountville's Veterans Home of California — an organization that, at that time, took care of the widows and orphans of servicemen. They attended Sacramento's monthly USO meetings to serve home-cooked Mexican food. They even assisted with the burial services of Mexican American soldiers who were killed in action.

The service of Las Madres Mexicanas de Guerra didn't stop with the war's end, however. Soon after, the women began selling pan dulce, tamales and raffle tickets to raise yet more funds — this time for a monument to honor all Mexican Americans who served America in World War I and World War II.

Once the women had raised $4,000, they commissioned a statue. It was sculpted in the likeness of a soldier — specifically, Enriqueta's son Joe — and named "El Soldado." And in 1951, it was installed at El Centro Mexicano de Sacramento (the Sacramento Mexican Center) — an organization Enriqueta had co-founded in 1948 with Phil Zúñiga. The community center was a physical symbol of Mexican American pride and fellowship in California's capital, and "El Soldado" represented the contributions of the community to American society.

The Sacramento Mexican Center closed its doors in 1975, and since then, "El Soldado" has stood guard over the State Capitol building. The statue was rededicated in 2017 and was given a new plaza with a more elaborate pedestal, listing scores of Mexican American Medal of Honor recipients. Every year, it is the site for California Mexican American Veterans Day ceremonies.

To this day, "El Soldado" stands as a reminder for all that Enriqueta did for her community. The reverence and respect for Enriqueta Andazola, by those who remember, remains strong. After her death in 1980, one eulogy at her funeral summarized the feelings of many friends and family: *"La pionera de nuestra colonia Mexicana."*

Dr. Margaret Chung

DEFYING STEREOTYPES was a lifelong pursuit for Margaret Chung. She defied them when she became the first American-born Chinese woman to become a doctor. She defied them when she opened the first Western clinic in San Francisco's Chinatown. And she subverted them in her personal life, whether she was donning masculine clothes, or taking care of countless "military sons." Margaret's consistently unconventional approach to life didn't just make her fascinating, it made her enormously popular.

Margaret was born in Santa Barbara in 1889, the oldest of 11 children. Her mother had been trafficked from China to San Francisco in childhood and was rescued by the Presbyterian Mission House in Chinatown. At 12, Margaret started work herself, slogging her way through long, grueling shifts at a restaurant. She battled her way into a prestigious private high school by winning a competition to sell the most *Los Angeles Times* subscriptions, thereby earning herself free tuition.

Margaret went on to attend medical school at the University of Southern California, one of only two women in her class during most of her time there. It was there that she first began wearing men's suits, and she was also responsible for founding the university's first medical sorority. Margaret's ultimate goal was to become a Presbyterian missionary. She admired the women who'd rescued her mother from a life of servitude and wanted to use her medical training to be of even greater service. But after graduation, her plans were foiled by racist policy. Her three applications to become a medical missionary were turned down solely because she was of Chinese descent.

To make matters worse, Margaret also struggled to get a hospital internship because of her gender. She went to work instead as a surgical nurse in Chicago, and it was there that she found the Mary Thompson Hospital — an institution specializing in the care of female patients by female doctors. After three years interning there, she moved on to Los Angeles's Santa Fe Railroad Hospital in 1916, where she became an accomplished surgeon.

Margaret's move to San Francisco came in 1921. "There were no Chinese doctors practicing American medicine and surgery in Chinatown," she noted later, "and I thought I saw a great future here." She opened her office on Sacramento Street. Once Margaret's practice was successful, she began the business of transforming healthcare in Chinatown. She volunteered at a local school, teaching and giving free wellness checks to scores of children. Then, in 1925, she co-founded the Chinese Hospital and helmed the Gynecology, Obstetrics and Pediatrics unit.

As Margaret became a well-known local figure, scandalous rumors spread about her loose morals — she was known to date both women and men, and many of them were white. While this prompted some of her more old-fashioned patients to abandon her care, her reputation attracted lesbian couples who could not be open about their relationship status at other medical offices. In addition, her reputation as a thoroughly modern woman — she drank in speakeasys and was often seen zipping around the city in flashy sports cars — also attracted women seeking birth control, sterilizations and abortions. While Margaret did not perform the latter, she offered referrals to trustworthy doctors who did.

"Around Dr. Margaret Chung has clustered the glamour and romance of both east and west," an issue of the *Californian* noted in 1934. The article also said that "every inch of wall space" in her consultation room was covered by signed photos of her most famous patients. They included Greta Garbo, Clark Gable and Joan Crawford.

It was a chance encounter, however, that would raise Margaret's public profile the most. In 1931, after Japan invaded Northeast China and bombed Shanghai, a member of the U.S. Navy Reserves, Steven G. Bancroft, approached Margaret to see if she knew a way for him to join the Chinese military. She didn't. But, taking a shine to Bancroft, she invited him and six friends — all pilots — over for dinner. Margaret hit it off with the men to such a degree that they were soon all eating, camping and hunting together on a regular basis.

One night, joking with Margaret, one of the pilots said, "You're as understanding as a mother . . . but hell, you're an old maid and you haven't got a father for us." Margaret replied, "Well, that makes you a lot of fair-haired bastards, doesn't it?" It was a moniker that stuck. And as word spread about "Mom Chung" and the "Fair-Haired Bastards," the group became a sort of social club.

By 1937, Margaret had more than 500 "sons" serving in the RAF, Army, Navy and Marines, and by the end of World War II, there were over 1,500. She provided maternal love and support, often feeding and housing them before and after missions. She gave each of them a small jade Buddha pendant, as a means to recognize one another while serving overseas, and she sent care packages and daily letters to raise their spirits.

Margaret's figurative adoptions of so many servicemen attracted positive press attention, and raised her profile enough to enable huge strides in her charitable campaigns. She co-founded Rice Bowl Parties — fundraising festivals held in 700 cities that went on to raise the equivalent of over $3 million today as aid sent to China. She also helped create the Women's Naval Reserve, co-founded the San Francisco Disaster Station and volunteered on its staff, and was an active member of the Red Cross. In 1942, one newspaper called her "San Francisco's Number One United States citizen."

After the war, Margaret continued to look after her "sons" as they adjusted back to civilian life, and her door remained open to them all until her death in 1959. When she died of ovarian cancer at 69 years old, Mayor George Christopher was one of her pallbearers.

Elaine Black Yoneda

WHEN AUTHORITIES INFORMED HER that her three-year-old son would be imprisoned in a concentration camp for the crime of being half Japanese, Elaine Black Yoneda — a white Jewish woman — insisted on going with him. Her Japanese American husband Karl was already being detained at Manzanar, a camp in the desert at the foot of the Sierra Nevada mountains. Now, just as the Yonedas had adjusted to the idea of a long period of separation, they would live as a family once more — albeit behind barbed wire.

"It was so ironic," Elaine later told a *People's World* journalist. "Only a few weeks earlier, I had been delivering soapbox speeches denouncing Nazi Germany for imprisoning Jews in Dachau. Here I was, a month later, demanding that I, a Jewish woman, be placed in a concentration camp."

It was not the first time in her life that Elaine had found herself incarcerated. Her activism on behalf of the Communist Party and unions had landed her behind bars more than once in the 1930s — most notably for her activities during San Francisco's notorious General Strike in 1934. That year, Elaine was arrested on charges of vagrancy and disturbing the peace at a Communist Party meeting of several hundred people at San Francisco's Jefferson Square. At the time, she was acting as an official for the International Labor Defense and as secretary of the Marine Workers' Industrial Union. Elaine made it a point to attend such meetings and demonstrations with copies of the Bill of Rights on her person. ("I could quote [them] verse and chapter," she later noted.)

Within one week of her arrest and incarceration, Elaine was on a hunger strike alongside Margaret Marshall, the lone other woman arrested that day. An image printed by the *San Francisco Examiner* on August 6, 1934, showed the women sitting side by side, facing each other and pointedly away from food that had been placed on a table in front of them. A caption noted that "each [woman] has [a] different view on proper methods of showing their contempt."

Elaine's activities in support of workers' rights were well established by that point. Born in New York City in 1906 to Russian Jewish immigrants who had fled Mazyr to escape pogroms and conscription in the czar's army, Elaine was raised with resistance in mind. In 1931, she moved to Los Angeles and joined the Communist Party.

By 1933, Elaine was in San Francisco, a city well known for its unionization efforts. Elaine quickly earned the nickname "The Red Angel" for regularly bailing out trade unionists and Communist Party members from jail. (She met her husband Karl while getting him released after his arrest and beating at a labor demonstration.) After two trials related to her high-profile 1934 arrest, the charges against Elaine were finally dismissed. "They are not vagrants. They are Communists," the appellate court judge ruled. By 1939, Elaine had become a powerful public speaker "out of necessity," and was campaigning to be elected to San Francisco's Board of Supervisors — a bid that was ultimately unsuccessful.

In 1953, Elaine was named during Senator Joseph McCarthy's Un-American Activities hearings. By then, the Yonedas were operating a farm in Cotati, but her political activities hadn't ceased and never would. From the late 1950s until her retirement in 1973, Elaine worked as a clerk for the International Longshoremen's and Warehousemen's Union Pacific Maritime Association pension fund.

During a life spent entrenched in the struggle for workers' rights, Elaine always spoke about her challenges in a manner that was matter-of-fact. While talking about what it was like to be a prominent member of the Communist Party during a period when sexism was rampant, she explained:

> The party's principles and everything was against the domination of male chauvinism, as the terms of equality. And you found women in various posts, not only in the district offices, but in the national office and on the newspapers. . . . But there was male chauvinism in the ranks and even in some of the leaders because it was too new a concept for some of them. . . . I would point out: "Now, look, first of all, I am a comrade. . . . You know you are committing a crime against your own constitution, your own principles. You're committing an act of male chauvinism.

Though Elaine is often remembered for her bravery as one of the few non-Japanese spouses imprisoned at an American concentration camp in World War II, she later spoke about the experience with some regret:

"Although I knew [Japanese internment] was a violation of basic human rights, I didn't speak out against it," she said. "I didn't raise my voice in protest. And in fact, I even thought for a period that they weren't really concentration camps, because to me, a concentration camp is the ovens . . . Once we were in camp, we did ask for some sort of hearings so that those who wanted to fight the actions would be given that opportunity to actively fight it."

Elaine and her son were ultimately released after her husband Karl enlisted in the U.S. military's intelligence service as a Japanese language specialist. For years after the war, the Yonedas campaigned for Japanese reparations, traveling regularly to the Manzanar site to raise awareness.

Elaine remained a powerful union figurehead until her death in 1988, and in the end, that is her true legacy.

"We believe in minority parties," Elaine once said. "If you let the big shots run the country, what will happen to us?"

Tsuyako 'Sox' Kitashima

THE KATAOKA FAMILY managed to hang on until May of 1942. It was then — three months after Franklin D. Roosevelt had signed Executive Order 9066 — that they were forcibly removed from their home in Alameda County and thrown into a prison camp. Across the United States, 120,000 innocent Japanese Americans and Japanese residents were suffering the same fate, more than 8,000 of them from the Bay Area.

The Kataokas were strawberry farmers from Centerville, a region that, today, is part of Fremont. Mom Yumi and her six children — three girls, three boys — had grown even closer since the death of her husband, Masajiro, just two years earlier. But their indefinite incarceration would test the family like never before.

Yumi's fifth child, Tsuyako, was 23 at the time of their imprisonment and already a hard worker — she worked on the family farm, on a local apricot farm, and in a doctor's office. Tsuyako had earned the nickname "Sox" as a child — the result of her peers pronouncing her name incorrectly. For her, the family's arrival at the Tanforan racetrack in San Bruno, where they would be forced to sleep in filthy horse stables, was the most humiliating moment of her life. Tsuyako shared one stable with her mother and brothers, while her sisters and their families moved into a neighboring one. Before their imprisonment had even begun, the family had been forced to euthanize their dog and sell off their most prized possessions — including Tsuyako's beloved piano.

After four months in Tanforan, the Kataokas were moved to a "relocation center" in Topaz, Utah. Conditions were dire in Topaz too, but it was there that Tsuyako evolved into a force to be reckoned with. She became an assistant block manager and acted as a messenger between residents and the camp's government officials. And, for the three years she spent there, she fought for better conditions for inmates.

Within the first year, however, her entire family — except for one sister — was transferred to a different camp at Tule Lake in Oregon. The separation from her family served to strengthen the relationship between Tsuyako and her boyfriend, Tom Kitashima, who was also imprisoned in Topaz. On August 11, 1945, the couple married in the camp. And just over a month later, they were finally released.

With little to return to in Centerville, the newlyweds moved to an apartment on Bush Street in San Francisco. Tsuyako's new lines of work reflected her continuing desire to be of service. She worked at both the War Relocation Authority and the San Francisco Veteran's Administration, stopping only to raise her son during the 1950s.

After her retirement in 1981, having lost her husband six years prior, Tsuyako threw herself even further into public service. She began volunteering with local organizations that were dear to her heart. One of her favorites was Japantown's Kimochi Inc., which, to this day, dedicates itself to assisting thousands of seniors, both in its facility and in their own homes. Later, Tsuyako also served on the city's Commission on Aging Advisory Council.

It was when she became the spokesperson for the National Coalition for Redress and Reparations that Tsuyako's dedication to good causes began to have a national impact. She took lobbying trips to Washington, D.C., made public speaking appearances to talk about life in the camps, and spearheaded letter-writing campaigns. During one of those, she personally mailed over 8,000 letters to both President Ronald Reagan and Congress. "It has been very exciting for me," she said in an interview at the time. "I treasure every letter that I fold and put in the mailbox."

It took years of non-stop pressure, but President Reagan finally signed the Civil Liberties Act into law in 1988. Two years later, the first financial compensation was received by Japanese American families. Checks for around $20,000 arrived, along with a letter of apology from President George Bush.

"A monetary sum and words alone cannot restore lost years or erase painful memories," Bush wrote. "We can never fully right the wrongs of the past. But we can take a clear stand for justice and recognize that serious injustices were done to Japanese Americans during World War II."

In 1998, Tsuyako's lifelong commitment to her community earned her a Free Spirit Award from The Freedom Forum ("dedicated to free press, free speech, and free spirit"), as well as a respect and admiration that stretched far beyond the Japanese-American Bay Area community.

"I have often called Sox the godmother of San Francisco Japantown because she took care of so many people in the Japanese American community and the Asian American community," said Carole Hayashino, President & Executive Director of the Japanese Cultural Center of Hawaii. "She was also an educator for our children. She spent a lot of time talking to students, sharing her experiences and the lessons of the Japanese American internment experience."

After her death in 2006 at the age of 87, Tsuyako "Sox" Kitashima's memorial was held at the Japanese Cultural and Community Center of Northern California. The online guest book speaks volumes about the number of lives she touched during hers.

"I had the good fortune to meet Sox through an oral history program we developed at the school where I taught. Sox was a phenomenal resource," wrote Larry Boston.

Regan Young of Alameda said: "Mrs. K . . . will always be my Pack 58 cub scout den mother, and the person who made sure the Jigoku's/Wong's Bait Shop/Angel's softball teams never went hungry!"

Joane Chiedi sent best wishes from Washington, D.C.: "Her energy and dedication to public service is an example for all to follow. She will truly be missed."

Frances Albrier

IN 1940, AN INDUSTRIALIST NAMED Henry J. Kaiser was approached by the British government and asked to build ships to aid the United Kingdom's World War II efforts. Kaiser was one of the main contractors responsible for building the Hoover Dam, and to accommodate the U.K.'s request, he opened his first shipyard in Richmond, California. As the war ramped up, one shipyard turned into four, and by war's end the workers in Richmond had built 747 ships — more than any other shipyard in America.

By 1942 the U.S. had entered the war as well, and with so many men away in the service, this Richmond hub was employing tens of thousands of women. That year, they hired their first Black female welder: Frances Albrier. At 44, Frances had already done her part for the war effort, volunteering with the Red Cross as a nurse and first aid instructor. But presented with any opportunity to contribute to a collective good, the Berkeley resident always grabbed it with both hands.

In addition to her nursing and shipbuilding, Frances also volunteered at Oakland's De Fremery Park Hospitality House, a recreation center for soldiers. During this time, she frequently used the letters pages of local newspapers to ask the public for donations that would benefit soldiers stationed all over the Bay Area. (At one point, she successfully acquired two pianos for a Berkeley camp of servicemen — one for church services, one for downtime.)

Frances was particularly concerned about the welfare of Black soldiers. After an incident of violence against Black servicemen stationed in Louisiana in 1942, Frances wrote an impassioned plea to the *Oakland Tribune*. Her letter said, in part:

> The Army has taken thousands of Negro men from the Northern, Eastern and Western sections and placed them in localities whose traditions and practices are to insult, beat, shoot and lynch them. . . . Fair minded, liberal Christian white Americans should help their brothers of darker skin by protesting against these insults heaped on citizens who are doing their part to save our democracy.

Frances's commitment to assisting the communities around her did not start — nor stop — with the war. Raised in Tuskegee, Alabama, by her grandparents after her mother's death, she graduated with a B.A. from Howard University in 1920. Frances moved to Berkeley that year and, inspired by an Oakland meeting of Marcus Garvey's Universal Negro Improvement Association, she volunteered as a Black Cross Nurse. The Black Cross was a Red Cross–inspired organization specifically focused on the health needs of the Black community at a time when hospitals and medical offices were still segregated, including in California.

Soon after that, during a five-year employment as a maid, manicurist and ticket-taker with Pullman Company first-class trains, Frances helped her fellow maids and porters to unionize.

In 1938, Frances served on the board of directors of the National Negro Congress and became the first woman elected to the Alameda County Democratic Central Committee. That same year, Frances was president of the East Bay Women's Welfare Club, which campaigned to employ more Black teachers in Berkeley schools. The club was also trying to get some Black representation in local government — which led Frances, in 1939, to become the first Black person to run for Berkeley City Council.

"I didn't think I would be elected," she said in 1977. "My idea of running was to meet the people. I knew that if I ran for city council, I would be invited to the clubs and organizations to give my views on the city government." Frances went on: "I wanted to tell them that we had 5,000 [Black] taxpayers without any representation in the city government or the schools of Berkeley."

Throughout the 1940s, ’50s and ’60s, Frances held prominent positions at an astonishing number of organizations, including the NAACP, the California Association of Colored Women’s Clubs, the Citizens Employment Council and the Golden Gate Democratic Club. Her motivations for being involved in so many different causes were reflected in one “thought of the day” notecard she wrote to herself in the late 1940s: “We have prayed together during the stirring, anxious, tragic years of war,” she wrote in neat cursive. “Now we have peace and we are profoundly grateful to God. We must, however, continue to pray with the same earnestness, the same faith and constancy. The problems of peace are many, as serious and as disturbing as those of wartime.”

The fire that drove Frances never cooled. As she approached her senior years, she became concerned about the welfare of the elderly — particularly those who were impoverished and did not have families to fall back on.

In 1965, Frances was appointed to the City of Berkeley’s Committee on Aging. She acted as a senior community representative at the Berkeley Senior Center. By 1971, she’d been called on to serve as a delegate at the White House Conference on Aging. Frances spent five years on the board of directors for the South Berkeley Model Cities Neighborhood Council, and in that role she was key in establishing Harriet Tubman Terrace — housing for low-income seniors. Frances even delivered meals (and companionship) to the elderly and infirm — something the City of Berkeley recognized with an award in 1978.

After a life thoroughly well-lived, Frances Albrier died on August 21, 1987. She left behind 11 grandchildren, 15 great-grandchildren and too many admirers, friends and supporters to count. Before she was buried at the Sunset View Cemetery in her beloved Berkeley, her family paid tribute to the incredible impacts Frances made in her 88 years.

“She served as a role model and inspiration for innumerable educators, politicians and community service groups,” they wrote. “It might be said of Frances Albrier that she was a living example of the philosophy ‘Be all you can be.’”

Elena Zelayeta

IT WAS THE STRANGEST OF RESTAURANTS. After climbing up to the top-floor flat of a Green Street apartment building, diners were asked to leave their coats in a bedroom, walk through the kitchen, and take a seat in one of four small, separate dining rooms.

Still, customers came from all over San Francisco, lining up in the hallway for a chance to eat Elena Zelayeta's food. Her cheese-stuffed green peppers, enchiladas and chilies rellenos were the stuff of legend. And, if not for the Great Depression, there's a good chance no one outside of her family would ever have tasted them.

In 1930, Elena was working as a secretary and her husband of five years, Lorenzo, was employed as a structural engineer. When the market crashed, they both lost their jobs and had to scramble to support their four-year-old son, Lawrence. Elena came up with the idea of opening a restaurant. She had first learned to cook from her Spanish mother and the chefs who worked at her parents' hotel in a small mining town on the outskirts of Pachuca, Mexico, and had honed her culinary skills carefully after getting married.

When Elena invited the public into her home to dine, the 32-year-old took on a punishing schedule. She worked seven days a week, rising at 5 a.m. each day and working until midnight. It wasn't easy — Mexican cuisine was not yet popular with white diners, and hostilities toward Latinos were at an all-time high during the national work shortage. But Elena's cooking skills were enough to silence the skeptical and attract a diverse group of customers. At her restaurant's peak, she prepared and served over 100 meals a day.

Within three years of opening her apartment doors, Elena's popularity had outgrown the space, and she reopened in a more formal setting, the King George Hotel near Union Square. This time the restaurant had a name: Elena's Mexican Village. Elena herself was known to emerge from the kitchen, greet people and dance joyfully through the dining room, much to customers' delight.

A twist of fate arrived in 1934. Elena had been left with permanent eye damage after a bout of scarlet fever as an infant, and the popular chef noticed she was having trouble focusing her eyes. Elena finally saw a doctor, who told her the situation was hopeless. A detached retina and severe cataract were about to render her blind, and there was no way to stop it. Compounding Elena's fears at the time was something else — she was pregnant.

As Elena lost her sight, she fell into a deep depression. A few days after going completely blind, in total despair, she attempted to throw herself from her seventh-story apartment window. Lorenzo caught her in the act and pulled her back from the ledge. Two months later, her second son was born.

The period after going blind was a tough one. When she left the restaurant in the hands of other chefs, diners slowly stopped coming. At home, Elena was learning how to live without sight while fighting off her depression. "For two years I was in the dark," she said in a 1944 interview. "Then I said to myself, 'Elena, you aren't being anything but a burden to your family.' So I changed."

Gradually, Elena taught herself to cook again, relying on her sense of touch and smell to remaster her favorite dishes. She timed how long things had been in the oven based on radio programming. She started inviting guests over, and attended movies and dances. She found silver linings in her sight loss. "To me, people cannot age," she said later. "I can see them as I saw them 10 years ago. Young, pretty, never growing old."

In 1944, Elena turned a major corner. She began teaching cookery classes at the San Francisco Center for the Blind. That same year, the chef wrote and released her first book, *Elena's Famous Mexican and Spanish Recipes*, which included many of the dishes she had served in her restaurant. The book was an immediate success and went on to sell half a million copies.

Elena's status as the only blind cooking teacher in the United States meant that her skills stayed in demand. At the invitation of the Mexican government, she visited Mexico City and established a rehabilitation program for people who had lost their vision. She also traveled all over America teaching blind students how to prepare their own meals.

Sadly, in 1945, tragedy struck once more when Lorenzo was killed in a catastrophic auto collision. Elena's grief, recovery and her experiences teaching blind students inspired a second book, *Elena's Lessons in Living*, published in 1947.

By 1950, Elena was considered the foremost authority on Mexican cooking in America. So it made sense when a brand-new San Francisco television station, KGO-TV, asked her to host her own show. For 15 minutes every Friday, *Fun to Eat with Elena* announced its arrival with a catchy jingle and an image of her two books. The methods used to circumvent Elena's disability were crude: The crew attached strings to her ankles and pulled on them to let Elena know which direction to turn for the camera.

Elena's ambitions didn't stop there. In 1951, she opened Elena's Food Specialties, a frozen food enterprise. Three more cookbooks followed. In 1952, *Elena's Fiesta Recipes* featured dishes she cooked for her own family. In 1958, *Elena's Secrets of Mexican Cooking* was hailed as the "definitive volume on the subject" by the *New York Times*. It was 1967 when *Elena's Favorite Foods, California Style* appeared, and somehow, Elena also found time to write a memoir, titled simply *Elena*.

Elena Zelayeta died in 1974 at the age of 76, having lived her life as the very picture of creative resilience.

"Many of us want everyone to adjust to us," Elena said in a 1950 interview. "We should begin with ourselves. There is little we can do about others. But there is much we can do to improve ourselves."

Louise Lawrence

SHE WAS AN ORGANIZER WHO PROVED invaluable to an entire generation of trans people. She helped to launch a magazine by and for gender-nonconforming people. She's the reason Dr. Alfred Kinsey's landmark research into human sexual behavior included individuals living beyond the binary. And she never once stopped to take credit for any of it.

Her name was Louise Lawrence.

Born in 1912, Louise tried for the first 30 years of her life to embrace being "Lew." She found work as a bank clerk at the age of 18, and married twice — first in her teens, then once more after the death of her first wife. It was only after her divorce that Louise fully embraced who she knew she was and began living full-time as a woman. And she moved from Berkeley to San Francisco to do so.

She had been quietly preparing for this moment for years. Even while married, she regularly scoured newspapers for reports about public cross-dressing, and then reached out to the people who'd been arrested. In addition, she placed personal ads in the backs of magazines to find other trans and gender-nonconforming people. Once in San Francisco, she made friends with drag performers at legendary North Beach club Finocchio's, and later got involved with the city's chapter of the Mattachine Society — one of the earliest LGBT organizations in America.

Such was her determination that, during a time when trans and cross-dressing people felt obliged to live secret lives, Louise openly began lecturing doctors at UCSF and assisting at its Langley Porter Clinic, with the goal of helping the medical profession understand that being transgender was not, in fact, a mental disorder.

Later, after Christine Jorgensen underwent high-profile gender affirmation surgery in Denmark in 1952, Louise was said to have remarked, "If only some of these American medical men could . . . not continually imagine that their own penis was removed when Christine's was, maybe we would see some sound thoughtful, imaginative progress made in this field."

Despite her frustration at not being able to break down barriers to healthcare more quickly, her work at UCSF is what led Louise to come into contact with Dr. Alfred Kinsey in 1948 — when he was the focus of national uproar for his book *Sexual Behavior in the Human Male.* Gender variance had been glaringly absent from the sexologist's landmark work, and Louise didn't just encourage Kinsey to include trans people in his follow-up — *Sexual Behavior in the Human Female* — she directly helped to facilitate it.

By then, Louise had built a network of almost 200 trans people across America and she decided to share some of their stories with Kinsey. She became invaluable to Kinsey, who employed her to transcribe life histories and interviews. Louise, in turn, provided Kinsey with trans stories and novels, as well as her own personal correspondence, diaries and scrapbooks "filled with articles about same-sex couples living as man and woman."

Louise also worked directly with pioneering sexologist Harry Benjamin, for whom she had an enormous amount of respect. Louise once described Benjamin as "one of the few medical men in this country who has any understanding of this problem." It was he who encouraged her, in 1951, to publish an article in the *International Journal of Sexology* titled "Transvestism: An Empirical Study." (Louise wrote it under the pseudonym Janet Thompson.)

Still, for Louise, it wasn't enough to merely reach the academics. In 1952, she co-founded the independent paper *Transvestia* with the aim of bringing wider "knowledge, acceptance [and] understanding" to the community. Importantly, it was Louise's extensive network of LGBTQ+ people that raised enough money to get the publication off the ground.

In the short documentary *Safety in Numbers: A Trans History*, Aaron Devor, chair of Transgender Studies at the University of Victoria, explains: "*Transvestia* became a lifeline for people to communicate with each other, to learn that there were others like them. It also had a section at the back where people could put in ads for pen pals . . . So they could build community in that way."

The impact of Louise's life of dedication to the LGBTQ+ community is vast. Not only is she remembered for leaving her door open to individuals who traveled to San Francisco seeking gender-confirming surgery, she is known to have counseled them too. It speaks volumes that both WPATH (the World Professional Association for Transgender Health) and Tri-Ess (an organization for heterosexual cross-dressers and their loved ones) are said to have been started in her kitchen.

To be labeled as transgender during the period Louise did her most outspoken work was to risk losing it all. Yet she never shied away from the difficult task of carving out space for herself and the multitude of others like her.

"I consider Louise to be my true identity even though the birth records say differently," she wrote in the 1950s. "And on this I will stand. For to me, as to most people who know me, I AM Louise."

STRIKE
to JUSTICE to PEACE
POWE to the PEOPL
QUAL IGHTS

Kartar Dhillon

IN A FRESNO HOSPITAL, just after giving birth to her first child, Kartar Dhillon was asked by a perplexed nurse why she was still using her maiden name. "Why don't you use your husband's name?" the nurse asked. Kartar — who also refused to wear a wedding ring — shot back without hesitation: "Why doesn't he use mine?"

It was the early 1930s, and though Kartar was still in her teens, she was not a person constrained by the expectations of her era. She would go on to become a dedicated unionist, a social justice organizer, a Black Panthers volunteer, a prolific writer and a passionate campaigner for India's independence. She also just happened to be the kind of live-wire that was always first on the dance floor at parties — especially if James Brown was playing.

Kartar learned resilience young. The fourth of eight children, born to Indian immigrants in Simi Valley in 1915, she spent her early childhood in Astoria, Oregon. Her adolescence was spent moving around California to communities that were not always welcoming.

"We definitely were not accepted," Kartar said in a 2001 interview. "They looked upon Sikhs and Indians generally as freaks as [if] we had come out of a circus of something. There was a great cruelty against our people."

Kartar graduated high school in 1932, when she was 17. Sadly, her mother died that same year and, having lost their father five years prior, she and an older brother were left to raise her younger siblings. When her brother suggested that Kartar might be better off moving to India, she opted instead to marry Surat Singh Gill, who had a degree in political science from U.C. Berkeley and was a passionate public speaker for the Gadar Party. He, like Kartar's entire family, was an active member of the group, which campaigned to free India from British occupation. (Her father was a Gadar Party founding member.)

Kartar's first daughter was born soon after her marriage. She later exclaimed that she was "so happy it was a girl because I wanted to prove to the world that she could be the equal of any boy ever born." She later had another daughter, and a son from Gill's first marriage also joined the family.

Life as a young mother was tough. The family lived in poverty, working as sharecroppers and sometimes day laborers. In the late 1930s, the family moved to Los Angeles, where Kartar worked as a waitress and, sometimes, a movie extra. She and her family relocated once more in 1940, to San Francisco — the place that she would call home for much of the rest of her life.

In 1942, Kartar's life opened up. She got divorced, later writing in an essay, "Freedom from marriage at the age of 27 with no job skills and three children to support is not quite the stuff of dreams, but I had finally taken my destiny into my own hands."

Kartar's earliest days of freedom were not quiet ones. As part of the World War II effort, the single mom worked as a machinist and as a truck driver, delivering servicemen to ports on their way to deployment. She developed a habit of sketching their portraits to send back to their families — a way to utilize her artistic skills while also showing compassion to those young men with uncertain futures.

After the war, Kartar was determined that she and her children would gain access to education and the arts. She studied art and literature to fulfill her personal passions, and shorthand and bookkeeping so she could better support her family. She scraped together money to take her kids to museums, lectures, plays and operas. She found donated tickets for symphony performances.

"I believed that life was meant to be enjoyed, not suffered," Kartar later wrote. "We may have lived in the slums at times, but our apartments were sunny with life."

Kartar's training enabled her to pivot into administrative work. She spent time working as a typist in an architect's office. She was a secretary for the Teamsters and a variety of other unions. She wrote for *People's World*, a workers' paper. When her own union — the Office and Professional Employees International Union — went on strike in the 1950s, she joined the picket lines.

In a 2001 interview, Kartar asserted:

> If we're born human, then we should have the same right to our two square feet on earth as anybody else — especially if we're workers. We don't have to worry about what would happen to the rich because they don't worry about us. . . . We have to fight back in any way we can because [the] world should belong to those who work.

Kartar's dedication to working people also found its way into her writing. The plight of immigrant workers was something she documented extensively — sometimes to devastating effect. Speaking once at Stanford University, she recounted the 1933 death of a baby who was refused care at a hospital simply because its mother had been in the county for less than 90 days — the requirement to receive medical aid.

By the 1970s, Kartar was living in Nob Hill with a beautiful view and rent she could only afford because her apartment had no kitchen. (She cooked over the fireplace and did the dishes in the bathtub.) Kartar was such a respected figure in the Bay Area by that point that in one 1972 newspaper ad urging the public to vote for McGovern instead of Nixon, her name appeared among scores of other trusted "working people." Another reason for her respect in the community was her volunteer work with the Black Panthers — she typed up the party's newsletter on weekends.

Kartar died in 2008 at the age of 93. Her childhood had begun thoroughly rooted in the ideas of the Gadar Party, and as she matured she was propelled toward every equality movement that crossed her path. As she wrote: "My sympathy remains forever with the underdogs of society, because I have never lost my place among them."

Marie Mason Potts

IN 1949, *SMOKE SIGNAL*, the first newspaper in California to be written, edited and controlled exclusively by Indigenous Americans, found itself with a new editor. It was a role that would transform the latter half of Marie Mason Potts' life. Marie took over just as a new, post-war wave of Native American activism was swelling. And what she did with the paper for the next 30 years would impact the lives of countless Indigenous people.

Smoke Signal had been founded in 1948 by Marie's youngest daughter, Kitty Flores, on behalf of the Federated Indians of California (FIC). When Kitty was forced to relocate for her husband's job, Marie — who already contributed to the paper — wasn't about to let *Smoke Signal* go out of print. She took over and remained dedicated to it for the rest of her life.

Smoke Signal's initial goal was to unify disparate Indigenous communities. "In Unity, There is Strength" its masthead declared, issue after issue. When its readers were struggling to deal with government officials or institutions, Marie sent them the forms they needed, instructions on how to file them and a list of official contacts who might be able to assist with land claims, civil rights issues and other legal battles. Marie's willingness to be so hands-on provided essential support for Native communities in California — but her impact was much wider.

The longer Marie worked on the paper, the more embedded she became in every aspect of Indigenous activism — something she had been involved with since her teens. But Marie recognized that writing about activism alone would not hold a large enough audience's attention. So alongside news, analysis and regular columns, she made sure *Smoke Signal* featured notices of obituaries, births and events — and, crucially, not a small amount of humor.

"An Indian was being interviewed for a position," one *Smoke Signal* joke read. "Among the questions asked was, 'Do you know a foreign language?' His reply was: 'Yes. English.'"

Marie knew the importance of levity during dark times, having endured plenty of her own. Born in Big Meadow, Plumas County, the ancestral lands of the Northern Maidu, Marie was the child of a Native woman who was raped by a white prospector. On the subject of her biological father and others like him, Marie once said, "They called the child a half-breed. I don't know why they were ashamed of fathering a child. But that's white society for you. My father was one of those sons o' bitches."

At five years old, Marie was forcibly enrolled — terrified and convinced she would be murdered — at the government-operated Greenville Indian School. She attended alongside several cousins and her older sister and brother. (The three siblings were given the last name Mason while attending.) By the time Marie had graduated from Pennsylvania's Carlisle Indian Industrial School in 1915, she had no homeland to return to. Big Meadow had been submerged under a new hydroelectric reservoir, Lake Almanor.

Marie never recovered from the loss of her homeland. But she captured its splendor in *The Northern Maidu*, a book she wrote in 1971 to leave a permanent record of how her people had lived.

> How wonderful it was, lying awake at night sometimes, to hear the coyotes bark and the hoot owls uttering their calls among the trees. Sometimes there would be the running clatter of squirrels on the bark slabs above us; and in spring and summer, just as it grew light before the sun rose, there came the enchantment of the bird chorus, the orchestra of the Great Spirit all around us. That clean pine smell on the morning wind — where can we find it now?

Shortly after graduation, Marie married Hensley Henry Potts, of the Konkow nation. ("A branch of the Maidu, but we didn't speak the same Indian language," she later explained.) Raising children would dominate the next two decades for Marie.

Once her children were grown, Marie had more time to dedicate to her personal passions. She moved to Sacramento in 1942 and went to work lecturing at Sacramento State about her heritage, Native American history and cultural preservation. She gave speeches all over the country about Indigenous issues, at civic organizations, churches and youth groups.

Marie's commitment to *Smoke Signal* spurred on her activism everywhere else. Starting in 1950, she chaired the "Indian exhibit" at the California State Fair. During the Korean and Vietnam Wars, she ensured Native American veterans, and those still fighting overseas, received free copies of the newspaper. In the '60s, she was western regional vice president of the California League for American Indians, an organization that helped Indigenous people access higher education. She also assisted the National Congress of American Indians with their community outreach and activism. She planned and attended countless Indigenous conferences, providing detailed summaries in *Smoke Signal.*

When her grandson took part in the occupation of Alcatraz, Marie spent time on the island and actively assisted the occupiers. She printed their "Proclamation to the Great White Father and All His People" on the front page of *Smoke Signal,* along with a list of supplies that the group needed.

Marie understood that joy and revelry were useful tools in the struggle. In addition to traveling with Maidu dancers to demonstrate traditional dances and explain their significance to others, Marie also enthusiastically assisted in bringing back the annual Bear Dance. In her book *The Northern Maidu*, she explained:

> From ancient times, the Maidu observed a Spring ceremony which took place when the first edible shoots came through the ground. . . . The grizzly bear was a symbol of life to us. If he had survived the winter, so had the tribe.

In June 1978, after traveling to a traditional Bear Dance in Janesville, Marie passed away at the age of 83, just 25 miles from her birthplace.

Esther Gulick, Kay Kerr and Sylvia McLaughlin

THE *OAKLAND TRIBUNE* STORY set off alarm bells across the region. Published April 23, 1961, "Our Shrinking Bay" dared to gaze 40 years into the future at what the Bay Area would look like if urban development continued unchecked.

"By 2020," Ed Salzman wrote, "the Bay could be little more than a wide river. Berkeley would extend so far west that part of the city would be in San Francisco County. And much more of the southern Eastbay shoreline would belong to San Mateo County."

It wasn't a work of Ed's imagination. The journalist had recently seen a paper the Army Corps of Engineers had written for the Department of Commerce. It explained in some detail that 70 percent of the Bay was less than 18 feet deep — meaning it could be filled and paved over relatively easily. Not only were plans afoot to start that process, but at the time there were no rules against such development. The private companies who owned the shoreline could do whatever they pleased with it.

Shortly after the *Tribune* published the article, Esther Gulick was visiting her friend Catherine "Kay" Kerr. They discussed Ed Salzman's story, and Kay asked Esther if she might have some time to work on preventing the decimation of the Bay. Esther said that she did, and the pair quickly started organizing, bringing in a mutual friend, Sylvia McLaughlin, who was eager to help as well.

None of the women had any idea they were about to embark on a lifelong journey.

In 1961, the San Francisco Bay was not in good shape. It had been a century since the Gold Rush, and at least 80 percent of the Bay's wetlands had been lost to development. The water was filthy, tainted by oil slicks, shipping pollution, trash from multiple garbage dumps at the water's edge and, worst of all, untreated sewage. At low tide, the stench emanating from the water wafted from Mill Valley to Oakland. At night, Esther, who had a view of the Bay from her Berkeley home, watched in horror as trash was dumped into the shallows and set on fire.

At first, Esther, Kay and Sylvia assumed they could join forces with an already established group that could help guide and inform their campaign. They invited every local environmentalist they could think of to Esther's home for a meeting. Those in attendance included reps from the Sierra Club, the Save the Redwoods League, Audubon and several local grassroots groups. They even invited author Harold Gilliam because of his work profiling the waterfront in his 1957 book *San Francisco Bay*.

After the trio had carefully laid out the urgent need for intervention, each of their attendees warmly agreed — then explained they were too busy with their own campaigns, and encouraged the women to start their own organization. To help, the Sierra Club's David Brower handed over his organization's mailing list and made himself available for advice.

That night, the Save the San Francisco Bay Association — now popularly known as Save the Bay — was born.

Almost half a century after he attended that first meeting, Harold Gilliam wrote for *SF Gate*: "My own feeling was that any attempt to stop the filling of the bay would be hopeless . . . I was certain that the three Berkeley women were too naive and inexperienced to realize the bay was as doomed as the orchards of the Santa Clara Valley."

Within two years, the association had proved Harold wrong, winning its first major victory. And it was a major one. Save the Bay almost single-handedly stopped the City of Berkeley from expanding into 2,000 acres of Bay waters.

Kay, Sylvia and Esther, it turned out, were a force to be reckoned with. They understood that the only way to win was to combine grassroots people power with irrefutable data. They consulted with biologists, engineers, economists, architects, legal scholars and city planners to prepare official arguments. They used flyer campaigns, phone chains and gatherings to attract more members to their cause. They charged $1 per year to receive their newsletter — a simple but effective way to fundraise.

It's hard to imagine now, but environmental campaigns were a fringe issue at the time. Kay, Sylvia and Esther instinctively knew how to take them mainstream. In 1968, for example, they distributed handmade "Save the Bay" flags to a parade of boats celebrating the start of yachting season. With this simple but savvy move they garnered press coverage without even having to organize a protest.

With attention, of course, came personal scrutiny. The women — and their supporters — were often subjected to mockery and name-calling. At one point, even an *Oakland Tribune* columnist piled on.

Through it all, Kay, Sylvia and Esther never stopped testifying at hearings, hassling government officials, petitioning state agencies and leading protests to Sacramento. All three steadfastly refused to be intimidated by the corporations, politicians, bureaucrats, landowners and occasionally journalists who attempted to block their path.

The tenacious organizing undertaken by these three women has influenced the ecology of the Bay Area in too many ways to comprehensively list. But it is thanks in large part to them that we have a state commission whose sole job it is to protect the San Francisco Bay. (The San Francisco Bay Conservation and Development Commission has been in place since 1965. And that, in turn, inspired the creation of the California Coastal Commission in 1972.) The environmental impact of the organization cannot be overstated.

Esther died in 1995. Both Sylvia and Kay died just months before their 100th birthdays, in 2016 and 2010 respectively. In a 1988 speech Sylvia noted: "Esther, Kay and I were inspired by the vision of what we felt San Francisco Bay could be and the reality of what was happening to it. We regarded the Bay as one of this country's national treasures and to us, and to many others, it was unthinkable that most of this beautiful natural resource could be filled."

Pat Maginnis

IN OCTOBER 1968, a reporter from the *San Francisco Examiner* spent an evening inside a third-floor office at 345 Franklin Street in San Francisco. By day, the place belonged to an attorney named Vincent Hallinan. After 7 p.m. every Thursday, Hallinan offered his office — free of charge — for America's very first post-abortion center.

The free clinic was a safe space for young women who'd recently undergone illegal abortions and weren't able see their regular doctors for post-operative care. It also offered free pregnancy tests, birth control prescriptions and advice from a Planned Parenthood volunteer. It was staffed by volunteer gynecologists, a nurse, a receptionist and a lab technician named Pat Maginnis.

It was Pat who had started the clinic, steadfast in her belief in a woman's right to choose. As she told a waiting room full of young women that night in 1968:

> Remember. Your abortion is your business and no one else's. You have a right to silence guaranteed by the Fifth Amendment. Abortions performed outside of the state are not reportable to police.

By the time the *Examiner* paid Pat's clinic a visit, she was already a well-known figure in San Francisco. In 1962, Pat had started the Society for Humane Abortion (SHA). In 1964, she co-founded the Association to Repeal Abortion Laws (ARAL), alongside Rowena Gurner and Lana Phelan Kahn. (It was a precursor to today's NARAL Pro-Choice

America.) Pat, Rowena and Lana were such a force to be reckoned with that they earned the nickname "The Army of Three."

The SHA and ARAL served different purposes, but enabled Pat and her likeminded campaigners to achieve goals on both an official and underground basis. Official operations included public campaigning and working diligently to change the laws of the day. Underground activities included the compiling and distribution of lists of safe abortionists, along with how much they charged. Pat and her colleagues held classes across the United States to teach women how to book an appointment, what to expect and how to prepare for the procedure. Other lessons taught women about reproductive health, anatomy, step-by-step instructions on how to perform abortions at home, and even the best ways to deal with police after an abortion. Bomb threats and protests were not uncommon outside these gatherings.

In the Bay Area, opposition came from an organization named Mothers Outraged at the Murder of Innocents (MOMIS) who protested outside events held by Pat, Rowena and Lana. MOMIS pushed district attorneys all over the region — San Francisco, Sacramento, Alameda, San Mateo, Sonoma and Santa Clara — to prosecute Pat, to no avail. By the end of the 1960s, local publications had started referring to her as "the Che Guevara of abortion reformers."

Pat's road to becoming the most prominent pro-choice campaigner of the 1960s was not an easy one. One of seven children, Pat was born in a small town outside of Oklahoma City in 1928. She was raised in dire poverty by a veterinarian father and a mother who endured chronic pain caused by giving birth so many times. ("My mother would tell you she enjoyed having children," Pat once said. "I didn't go through childhood with that impression.")

In 1950, Pat left a job at the Bureau of Mines and joined the Women's Army Corps, training as a surgical technologist. After being assigned to a pediatrics and obstetrics ward in Panama, she witnessed the aftermath of botched abortions and forced births. In 1966, she told the *Examiner*: "My first real contact with abortion was in the Army. A woman pregnant by another man and expecting her husband's return tried to abort herself

[and] was hospitalized. The poor thing, who received no sympathy or understanding, became so distraught, a wire cage was placed over her bed. She was held captive like an animal. I still shudder at the memory."

Pat left her three-year enlistment as a corporal and decided to attend San Jose State College under the G.I. Bill. During her studies there, she got pregnant three times. On the first occasion, she traveled to Mexico for an abortion. She administered the next two on herself at home. After one of them landed her in the hospital, she was asked if she had given herself an abortion. Her response? "Sure I did. Want me to demonstrate how in court?"

After Pat graduated in 1961, at age 33, she worked nights as a medical technologist. Her late schedule was by design — she needed her days free for pro-choice campaigning. That year, she was arrested for the first time for distributing literature that advised women how to access abortion services. At the time, it was a felony in California to "willfully compose and publish a notice and advertisement of a medicine and means for producing and facilitating a miscarriage and abortion." However, the judge at Pat's trial concluded that she had been arrested on grounds that were unconstitutional, and promptly set her free. "Now I can paper the town with leaflets," Pat joyfully announced after the verdict, "and that's exactly what I plan to do."

Eight years later, however, Pat found herself convicted of "willfully writing, composing and advocating abortion techniques." In 1966, she and Rowena were arrested in San Mateo after teaching an abortion class. They paid their fines and carried on, unrepentant. Pat told the *Examiner* shortly afterwards, "It kills me to see these young healthy women be expected to jeopardize their lives for what is a simple, safe surgical procedure."

Pat Maginnis died on August 30, 2021, at the age of 93, having spent her life in activism. (Her later interests included animal rights, gay rights and environmentalism.) Those present at Occupy Oakland in 2011 might recall Pat showing up to hand out pea soup. Of course, it was her dedication to women's health that Pat will always best be remembered for.

"These are personal matters, private matters. They don't concern others — not doctors or judges or boards," she told the *Rapid City Journal* in 1969. "Women have got to fight. They've taken this kind of vile abuse too long."

Rosalie Ritz

AFTER ROBERT F. KENNEDY'S assassin was put on trial in 1969, Rosalie Ritz shared a controversial opinion about the much-despised man. Rosalie, the sketch artist at Sirhan B. Sirhan's trial, described him as "the only honest man" in the courtroom. "It was my first experience with a revolutionary," she told the *Oakland Tribune* shortly after the guilty verdict came down. "Of course it was pointless — all killing is pointless. You have to be nutty to do it. But Sirhan knew exactly what he wanted to do and he did it."

The Sirhan trial was not the only time Rosalie came into close contact with a revolutionary. She spent the late 1960s and '70s covering the trials of Black Panthers including Huey P. Newton, Angela Davis and the Soledad Brothers. She also documented the high-profile prosecution of heiress-turned-"urban guerrilla" Patricia Hearst.

In fact, Rosalie was one of the most in-demand courtroom sketch artists of the era, providing illustrations for the Associated Press, CBS News, KPIX, KNXT and KQED. She was known to make up to 21 drawings a day and could sketch an entire jury in minutes. Rosalie was also an accomplished writer who took readers behind the scenes. One article she wrote for the *Los Angeles Free Press* used the Patricia Hearst trial to highlight the overzealous security Rosalie had experienced at similarly high-profile cases involving Black defendants.

Rosalie didn't just have a front-row seat to one of the most turbulent eras in Bay Area history — she had the talent and determination to share it with the rest of the world. "It's never as tough as you think it is," she once said, "if you act from strength, not from fear, and you speak the truth to power."

Rosalie was outspoken from a very young age — possibly the result of being the seventh of 10 children, all of whom lost their father at an early age. (Rosalie was just 9.) At 14, her prodigious artistic skills allowed her to attend art college in Milwaukee. At 16, she hit the road with her big sister's ID, alongside four other young women, and earned money for her family making portraits of people at circuses, fairs and other community events across the Midwest.

After graduating from Layton Art College, Rosalie married a Navy officer (and future accountant) named Erwin in 1946, and had four daughters. When her family relocated to Walnut Creek from Washington D.C., Rosalie was already established as a courtroom artist with a vibrant, vigorous style, having landed her first job at the Army-McCarthy hearings of 1954. Speaking to the *Oakland Tribune* 15 years after the fact, Rosalie recalled: "Somebody I knew there knew Joe McCarthy, so I went to his office and asked if I could attend his closed Senate hearings. I just started sketching while I was there and when I came out of the room, [a TV station] offered to buy the sketches. That started it."

What kept it going was Rosalie's tenacity. On the first day of Huey P. Newton's trial, she successfully talked her way into the courtroom, despite the fact that she'd not yet been issued a press pass. Later, she was permitted to visit Newton in a holding cell to draw him — a privilege not afforded to any other court reporters. It probably helped that she understood fundamentally what the Black Panthers were trying to do. "These were people who really believed in doing the right thing," she later said.

Aware of the importance of the moment, Rosalie was careful to retain ownership of all of her artwork. Though it would have earned her a better living, she never sold her courtroom sketches — only the use of them. After her death from lung cancer in 2008, Rosalie's will left more than 1,800 of her courtroom drawings to the Bancroft Library at U.C. Berkeley.

Away from the courtroom, Rosalie was passionate about making large-scale oil paintings and sculptures, and she always had an eye on the wider Bay Area art community. In 1974, she opened the Upstairs

Art Gallery at 927 Broadway alongside fellow artists, Thomas Bray and Edy Keeler. Rosalie recognized that the Bay Area arts scene — including the organizations responsible for handing out grants and funding — was focused almost exclusively on San Francisco, and she desperately wanted to change that.

"My opinion of Oakland is that it is a very beautiful city," Rosalie told the *Oakland Tribune* in 1974. "[Its neglect] is due to snobbery of people around Oakland, and we let them get away with it. What we're going to do is start saying 'The Oakland San Francisco Bay Area' and they'll complement one another."

Though the Upstairs Gallery was a scrappy endeavor once described by the *Tribune* as a "struggling, always dollar-short art colony above a pawn shop," Rosalie successfully made the impact on the arts scene that she had hoped for. In 1979, when the City of Oakland and the Labor Department awarded federal unemployment seed money to the Oakland art community for the first time, it went to Rosalie and the Upstairs Gallery. She used the $100,000 check to hire staff artists.

When the gallery was inundated with applicants, Rosalie pledged to help as many of the non-successful candidates as she could, seeking out other outlets that might offer art-related jobs in Oakland. "Oakland can't afford to lose them to other cities," she said.

In the end, Rosalie Ritz approached everything she did with a full-hearted determination that enabled her to live life on her own terms and in a way that sought to benefit others. Her uncompromising vision drove her to leave her mark on the world. At the end of her life, she knew that she had.

"It was a great ride," Rosalie said. "I always had a smile because I did what I wanted to do. I interpreted the world in drawings, in writing. I had a good time."

March Fong Eu

IN 1973, BEFORE AN AUDIENCE at Foothill College in Los Altos, March Fong Eu made a searing speech titled *The Self Sufficient Woman*. In it, she directed her gaze squarely at the patriarchy and despaired at the state of gender inequality in America.

"Maybe if some men had to bear and rear unwanted babies themselves, they would understand better our resentment of laws relating to our reproductive systems," she said. "Maybe if some men let their wives involuntarily control their income, they would understand better our resentment of present discriminatory statutes directed toward women as a class. And maybe if some men were raped, and, in pursuit of justice, they found that they had to reveal humiliating information about their past lives, maybe then they would understand the anger of women who feel they are doubly wronged by rapists and the laws concerning rape."

A first-generation daughter of Chinese immigrants, March spent her entire life working to smash down the barriers that women faced. And she was successful in that pursuit at every stage of her career.

First, she graduated from U.C. Berkeley. Then came a Master's from Mills. Finally, she earned her PhD at Stanford. In her first profession as a dental hygienist, March became the first woman and first Asian American to chair UCSF's Department of Dental Hygiene. Then, starting in 1956, March served three terms on the Alameda County Board of Education, serving as its president between 1961 and '62. In 1966, she won a place on the California State Assembly — with a margin of more than a million votes. Representing Oakland and Castro Valley, March was one of only two women serving on the 118-person assembly at the time.

"There is no argument to the opinion that this nation could benefit greatly by increased participation by women in decision-making positions," she later said. "We do bring to bear unique experiences and insights, unlike our male counterparts."

In 1969, March demonstrated that point when she went to war against pay toilets in public buildings. At the time, men's urinals were free to use, but stalls cost a dime to access. It was an early example of what we now refer to as the "pink tax" — the extra money women are forced to pay for products and services. March campaigned fervently for a statewide ban on the bathroom fee, using a combination of tenacity and humor.

The campaign culminated in a stunt on the steps of Sacramento's Capitol building, during which March smashed a padlocked toilet with a sledgehammer. She flung the sledgehammer with such gusto, assembled journalists were forced to duck out of the way. The speech she made that day was unabashedly filled with toilet humor too, much to the amusement of the press. ("The movement is on!" she declared with a cheeky smile. "The pressure is mounting!")

In the end, it took five years after March's toilet stunt for then-Governor Ronald Reagan to sign legislation banning pay toilets. It is unlikely to have happened at all without March loudly bringing the issue to the state's attention. She used that fact in her 1974 campaign to become Secretary of State. March would go on to win, with a record 3.4 million votes. (Four years later, she was so popular, that number had swelled to 4 million.) March was the first woman to hold the position and the first Chinese American elected to a constitutional office in California.

March's fortitude was tested in 1986 when an axe-wielding burglar broke into her home and brutally beat her. She survived, but was left with serious injuries that warranted a hospital stay. Her deputy, Anthony L. Miller. told the press at the time, "She's a real scrapper and survivor. She feels very lucky to be alive."

Mr. Miller, incidentally, was an openly gay man that March hired as Chief Deputy Secretary of State in 1980, saying she didn't want the support of anyone who might have a problem with his sexuality. "Things are much different today," he said in 2018, "because of people like March Fong Eu who led the way to tolerance."

March held onto the position of Secretary of State for almost two decades and, in that time, transformed voting access for Californians. She introduced voter registration by mail, absentee ballots for anyone who requested them (no reason needed), candidate statements on ballot pamphlets and internet reporting of election results.

While in office, March pushed for the various divisions of the Secretary of State's office to be consolidated under one roof. The resulting downtown Sacramento building has been named after her since 2019.

In 1994, President Bill Clinton named March U.S. Ambassador to Micronesia. She served for two years before resigning to assist in the Clinton–Gore election campaign. Though she never held a prominent office again, March never stopped pushing for what she felt was right. In the '90s, she spoke out against prejudice toward Asian Americans. After the 2000 Bush v. Gore election debacle, March took an axe to a punchcard voting machine at a Sacramento news conference.

March Fong Eu died in 2017 at the age of 95. The impact she made is almost impossible to measure — both on the careers of the female politicians coming up behind her and on the everyday lives of women statewide.

Perhaps March said it best herself during a 1979 interview: "Not too bad for a lady born behind a Chinese laundry."

Sofía Mendoza

IT WAS THE FIRST TIME anything like it had happened in the history of California.

When the clock struck 10 a.m. on April 26, 1968, 150 of Theodore Roosevelt Junior High's Mexican American students promptly stood up and walked out. They were protesting the racist treatment they had been subjected to by numerous teachers, and as they picketed loudly at the school gates, change began to feel possible.

One of the boys taking part in the protest that day was the son of Sofía Mendoza, a mom who had grown increasingly frustrated with the ways Chicano teens were being marginalized at the place that was supposed to be nurturing them. Sofía had heard first-hand the racial epithets some of the school's teachers used. She had been told by students that corporal punishment was being doled out along with the prejudice. She also knew that, in some classes, Mexican American children were given worksheets instead of the textbooks routinely provided to their white classmates.

First, Sofía documented the infractions as she heard about them. She then rallied other Latino parents to raise awareness about what was happening behind the school gates. When their complaints prompted little change, the parents encouraged their kids to take action.

Fred Hirsch, a labor rights leader and friend to Sofía, recalled in 2015, "Discrimination was the big issue. The tracking system that was enforced [at Roosevelt] put Latino kids at a disadvantage, especially immigrants and children whose first language was Spanish . . . . We had some small meetings, and through the meetings, the students learned that school funding was based on their attendance. They quickly understood they had economic power in just showing up — or not showing up."

Three days after the walkout, 500 students held a rally in the school's auditorium to discuss racist practices at the school. Both actions prompted an outpouring of support around East San Jose, and the school board was finally forced to take action. In quick succession, 36 teachers plus the junior high's principal and vice principal were fired.

"The students learned so much from their organizing," Sofía said. "They learned that they have every right to make changes without winding up in juvenile hall for being labeled as troublemakers."

Sofía's instinct for organizing was a product of her upbringing. Her father was a labor organizer in Arizona and Southern California, starting in the 1930s. "I was born into a lot of activity," she recalled in 2010. As a freshman, she objected to the fact that there was no Spanish Club at her Campbell high school and won the right to start one by organizing her fellow students. Her desire to make things better for Mexican Americans in East San Jose began after she moved there with her husband and the couple had their son, Willie, and two daughters, Linda and Saundra.

"Before I moved to East San Jose," Sofía once explained, "I heard that everybody that was bad lived in East San Jose. Everybody that was poor lived in East San Jose. The schools in East San Jose were no good. I never heard anything good about it. Never."

After the sweeping changes at Roosevelt, Sofía began to think about other ways that East San Jose could be improved. Law enforcement had been of great concern to her from the moment she moved there from Campbell.

"I had never seen so many cops driving by," she said in one 2010 speech. "In a matter of five years, cops had killed 16 people. Of course, most of them were Latino. We had no representation."

Sofía channeled her concerns into organizing a march to City Hall that attracted 2,000 people protesting what they saw as excessive use of force by San Jose's Police Department. In 1968, she was key in organizing a Community Alert Patrol (CAP) with a diverse group of other concerned citizens, including Tom Ferrito, who went on to become Mayor of Los

Gatos in 1980. It was essentially a sort of Neighborhood Watch — only, instead of keeping an eye out for the activities of criminals, volunteers kept watch over the police instead.

"We monitored all the police patrols," Sofía later explained. "We would send our cars that were equipped with two-way radios, cameras and tape recorders. Not to interfere, but only to document, so we could [use] the information [in] court. We had to go that far. We did get rid of the chief of police. That's when . . . there were a lot of good changes in the police department."

CAP's work ultimately led to the creation of the city's Office of the Independent Police Auditor, and Sofía became a member of the Independent Police Auditor Advisory Committee.

By the 1970s, Sofía was a well-established and much-loved force in her community. She battled San Jose's Redevelopment Agency when her neighbors were suffering mass evictions. She was active in helping Chilean refugees from the Pinochet regime to settle in the city, and in getting East San Jose its first health clinic. Like her father before her, she became involved in farmworker unionization. Sofía also led the Mexican American community in fighting for voting rights. Her campaigning even led to the reform of San Jose elections for city council members and introduced district representation, leading to a more diverse leadership.

Sofía never stopped being of service to the community. Later in life, she served as a social worker, a member of the board of directors at the Community Child Care Council, and a community organizer for the Family Service Association of Santa Clara County.

Throughout it all, Sofía retained an impressive sense of humility.

After her death in 2015 at the age of 80, Nannette Regua, a history teacher she had mentored, said of Sofía: "She never said, 'I did this.' She never said, 'I led these community organizers.' It was always, 'We.'"

Ruth Beckford

IN THE LATE 1960S, an energetic 43-year-old named Ruth Beckford was teaching an Afro-Haitian dance class in Oakland. A dancing pro since the age of eight, Ruth had a habit of taking a personal interest in her students. She taught the youngest ones a combination of life skills. She encouraged teens and young women to love themselves and pursue their dreams. And when one of her students told Ruth about her involvement with the Black Panther Party, Ruth was keen to be of assistance with that, too.

The student in question was LaVerne Anderson, who happened to be dating Huey P. Newton. In September of 1968, when the idea for the Panthers' Free Breakfast for School Children Program first came up, it was Ruth who sprang into action and made it happen.

Ruth had long been a parishioner at Oakland's St. Augustine's Episcopal Church. She approached her priest there, Father Earl A. Neil, to find out if St. Augustine's was willing to host a daily program to feed neighborhood kids. Father Neil agreed, and he and Ruth went about building a health-code-safe kitchen and dining space, as well as a nutritionally balanced menu.

On the first day — a Monday in January 1969 — 11 children came to eat. By Friday that number had swelled to 135. Ruth and Father Neil made such a success of the free breakfasts that the program was soon mandatory in all Black Panther chapters nationwide. It was also a shining example of Ruth's ability to turn ideas into action, and to plant seeds that would one day create mighty forests.

Ruth was born on December 7, 1925, in Oakland's Providence Hospital to a Jamaican father and a mother from Los Angeles. Ruth was the youngest of four and grew up in a household so supportive that when they saw her kicking along to music in her crib her parents pledged to get Ruth into dance classes as soon as she was old enough.

At three, Ruth began training in "every kind of dance." By eight, she was a vaudeville dancer. By 14, she was teaching other children. At 17, she toured with the prestigious Katherine Dunham Company, where she fully embraced African and Caribbean dance for the first time. Ruth loved the work but declined a seven-year contract from the company so she could attend U.C. Berkeley.

During her studies, Ruth was the only Black dancer in U.C. Berkeley's dance club, Orchesis, an experience that prepared her for working in majority-white companies later on. In her twenties, as the only Black dancer with the Anna Halprin and Welland Lathrop modern dance company, Ruth said she could sometimes hear the audience gasp as she arrived on stage.

Once Ruth had graduated, she started an annual modern dance showcase that ran for over a decade. Then in 1947, at just 21, Ruth started the Oakland Recreation Modern Dance Department — the first free, city-funded dance classes in the United States — and remained project director there for 20 years. By the time she left in 1967, the department was running 34 modern dance classes for 700 students of all ages and abilities.

Of the importance of this program, Ruth later stated: "The girls got a lot of doses of self-empowerment training, self-esteem training. Out of the thousands of girls that I taught, I knew a few would be dancers, but they all had to become women."

These relationships were so important to Ruth, she prioritized them over having children of her own. "I feel if I had had children," she said in 2000, "I would not have been the mentor to the hundreds and hundreds of girls I mentored."

Starting in 1954, Ruth ran her own company, the Ruth Beckford African Haitian Dance Company. Her understanding of traditional styles was so exhaustive, she was invited to choreograph a folk festival in Haiti in 1958. At home, her company's performances — comprised of six dancers accompanied by three drummers — were unlike anything most dance fans had seen in the Bay Area before. For a start, the company was comprised entirely of Black dancers.

After Ruth retired from teaching in 1975, she became an author, writing an autobiography, two cookbooks and a biography of Katherine Dunham. She also co-authored *The Picture Man*, about Black Bay Area photographer E.F. Joseph. Her final work, *Still Groovin'*, was a book of spiritual advice and affirmations aimed squarely at mature women. "Women are sort of out there by themselves," she said, "and women have to mentor each other."

Between 1984 and 1988, Ruth wrote a trilogy of plays titled *'Tis the Morning of My Life*, about a woman named Roxie Youngblood who finds herself in a relationship with a much younger man. Ruth admitted the story was inspired by her own life.

"I have a different energy, I think, to most men my age," she once explained. "As long as I have this energy, I'm going to use it and have fun with younger people. Younger men have the energy I have."

When a New York theater asked permission to stage her first play, Ruth agreed, but only if the original Bay Area cast could perform it. "It's time for New York to see what the West Coast can do," she insisted.

Later, Ruth served on the Board of Oakland's African American Museum and Library, where she founded an oral history program. She counseled homeless people in Berkeley, and women in shelters and prisons around the state. She served on a dance panel at the National Endowment for the Arts and campaigned for better theater facilities in Oakland. She even founded a women's golf club.

Ruth Beckford remained indefatigable until her death at age 93. Shortly before her passing on May 8, 2019, she reflected on a life thoroughly well lived.

"I have a joyous life, I have a good time," she said. "I choreographed my life. Step-by-step, year-by-year."

Del Martin and Phyllis Lyon

WHEN *LESBIAN/WOMAN* was released in 1972, the effect was seismic. Co-authors Del Martin and Phyllis Lyon dedicated their book to "daughters throughout the world who are struggling with their identity." They also wrote a clear, unequivocal explanation:

"A Lesbian is a woman whose primary erotic, psychological, emotional and social interest is in a member of her own sex."

That a book about lesbian culture would even require such a definition feels bizarre today. But the lifelong work of San Francisco couple Del and Phyllis is one of the reasons that so few people require such annotations now.

When Del and Phyllis began their relationship in 1952, America was a terrifying place to be LGBTQ+. Looking back later in life, the couple wrote an essay recalling the "climate of fear, rejection and oppression" that marked the earliest days of their 56-year romance. "Lesbians and gay men, if found out," the pair wrote, "were subject to reprisals from all quarters of society: employers, police, military, government, family and friends."

With that in mind — after moving in together on Valentine's Day 1953 — Del and Phyllis sought friendships with fellow lesbians outside of the oft-raided gay bars. That led to the establishment in 1955 of the Daughters of Bilitis (DOB), the first lesbian-rights organization in the U.S.

Originally the idea of Rosalie Bamberger, a local Filipina factory worker, the nonprofit started with just four couples. Del was the club's first president, and by the end of its first year, DOB had 15 official members. From there, the group expanded their ranks via the Daughters of Bilitis newsletter and, starting in October 1956, *The Ladder*, a groundbreaking lesbian magazine edited by Phyllis. She held a degree in journalism from U.C. Berkeley, and had worked in magazines and newspapers since the '40s — but here, she published under the pseudonym Ann Ferguson.

Phyllis's pen name wasn't the only reflection of the fear of being found out that marked the era: the name Daughters of Bilitis came from *Songs of Bilitis,* a collection of lesbian love poems published in 1894 by Pierre Louÿs, who claimed the text was based on ancient Greek scripts. If anyone asked, the women could say that DOB was merely a club for women who were passionate about Greek poetry.

What's more, in 1960, when the organization's first conference was held in the penthouse of San Francisco's Hotel Whitcomb, all attendees were careful to wear skirts and dresses, lest they be accused of cross-dressing. (They were right to do so: SFPD's "homosexual detail" showed up to see if anything nefarious was going on.) At one point, Del and Phyllis were so concerned about their office being raided and the DOB mailing list being exposed, they hid the document in the back of their station wagon.

Still, DOB persisted, acting as a support and social group, and as a source of information for its members. Even in the organization's earliest days, Del carried herself with an unrivaled fortitude. In 1959, she attended a Mattachine Society convention in Denver to voice her dissatisfaction with the gay organization's attitude towards women. Pointing out that the group was 99% male, Del announced from the stage: "Lesbians are not satisfied to be auxiliary members or second-class homosexuals. One of Mattachine's aims is that of sexual equality. May I suggest that you start with the lesbian?"

Del channeled that energy into her writing as well. Her first solo book, *Battered Wives,* was published in 1976, becoming the first American book to discuss domestic violence in depth. By then, Del was also the first out lesbian to have served on the National Organization of Women's board of directors. Phyllis was a fellow NOW member, which made them the first out lesbian couple to join.

The '70s were a time of great change for Del and Phyllis. Daughters of Bilitis and *The Ladder* both came to an unceremonious halt in 1970 because of intragroup politics and a couple of bad actors. Without either entity to pour their energy into, Del and Phyllis instead focused on writing *Lesbian/Woman* — and this time, with incredible bravery, they used their real names. A year later came *Lesbian Love and Liberation: The Yes Book of Sex,* a sex-positive guide that Del and Phyllis wrote to encourage tolerance, consent and frankness in the bedroom.

By 1979, the couple had established the Lyon-Martin Women's Health Center in San Francisco — a safe space for lesbian couples to receive healthcare. Today, the clinic is also focused on serving trans, nonbinary, gender nonconforming and intersex people.

Throughout the '90s, as LGBTQ+ people increasingly found acceptance in America, Del and Phyllis celebrated how far they had come in a series of interviews and essays, with the *San Francisco Examiner* referring to them as "the mothers of lesbian visibility."

In 2004, Del and Phyllis became the first same-sex couple to marry in San Francisco. The union was frustratingly short-lived — within a month, the California Supreme Court had declared the marriage invalid.

But four years later, Del and Phyllis proudly returned to City Hall and made things official once more, after the California Supreme Court's landmark decision on marriage equality. The couple were literally first in line, just as they had been in 2004, and were married by then-Mayor Gavin Newsom — the man who had sanctioned their first wedding.

It was an enormously meaningful day for the couple. When Del died at the age of 87, less than three months after their wedding, Phyllis said: "I am devastated, but I take some solace in knowing we were able to enjoy the ultimate rite of love and commitment before she passed." Castro's Pride flag and the flags at City Hall flew at half-staff in Del's honor.

Phyllis soldiered on without her love for another 12 years. She died in 2020, aged 95, at home in San Francisco. On learning of the news, Gavin Newsom tweeted: "Phyllis — It was the honor of a lifetime to marry you & Del. Your courage changed the course of history."

Violeta Marasigan

IN JANUARY 1970, Violeta "Bullet" Marasigan's husband implored her to not "bring any more work home."

Quoted in a *San Francisco Examiner* profile, Pete Marasigan was, the newspaper reported, only half-joking. Because when Violeta Marasigan brought the office home with her, it wasn't stacks of papers and files. More often than not, it was human beings that needed food or a bed for the night.

Violeta had been in non-stop action since 1968, when she was hired by San Francisco's United Filipino Association (UFA) as a social worker. Born in the Philippines in 1939, Violeta had moved to California to study at San Francisco State College. Shortly after graduation, the UFA brought her on to assist the elders — or manongs — of Manilatown, a 10-block stretch of Filipino businesses, restaurants and social hubs centered around Kearny and Jackson Streets in San Francisco. She was perfect for the position.

"I'm very optimistic," she later explained. "I think a lot of things can be done if we really put ourselves in it — [and] not half-heartedly."

There was nothing half-hearted about Violeta. She spent her entire life fighting for Filipinos, both in the Bay Area and abroad. Her nickname "Bullet" was coined while she was still in her teens; "Bolet" is a Tagalog version of the name Violeta, but her moniker morphed into "Bullet" once her friends realized how impossible it was to stand in her way.

"When I started working with the old men," she told the *San Francisco Examiner* in 1970, "I saw that they were discriminated against in terms of their access to social services. A lot of them had been here for over 30 years, but they could still barely speak English or write."

Violeta quickly deduced that most of these men — frequently World War II veterans — were not receiving all of the SSI benefits they were entitled to. Violeta took it upon herself to bring them in to the Social Security office and advocate for them, one by one, until they each received what they were owed. And they were owed a lot.

After the U.S. colonized the Philippines in 1898, Filipino men became a cheap labor source for American companies. In the 1920s, 100,000 workers arrived from the Philippines to work in the U.S. But not only were these men barred from bringing their families with them, by 1933 in California, they were also prohibited from marrying outside of their race.

With so many barriers to building a traditional family structure, it became essential for this first wave of manongs to form their own communities. Manilatown was central to that, and central to Manilatown was the International Hotel (often called the "I-Hotel"). The three-story structure at 838 Kearny Street housed 200 residents — mostly elderly and impoverished Filipino and Chinese men. The UFA's headquarters were situated directly next door.

In Autumn of 1968, Violeta and the UFA faced their biggest challenge yet. Residents at the I-Hotel began receiving eviction notices. (The owner of the property wanted to turn the hotel into a multi-level parking lot.) Residents, students and other civil rights groups banded together to keep the I-Hotel open, and Violeta was a key player in negotiating the hotel a new three-year lease.

Violeta couldn't have known that just four years later, the hotel would be sold to a developer. Then, on August 7, 1977, 400 police officers forced their way through a human chain around the I-Hotel and forcibly dragged out its residents, bringing an end to the hotel — and Manilatown itself — for good.

Violeta was not there to see the end of the hotel she fought so hard to save. She had returned to Manila in 1971, joining the resistance against Ferdinand Marcos. She proved herself once more to be an outspoken activist, visiting and raising money for political prisoners. For her trouble, she was arrested in 1982 on explosives charges.

Violeta spent a year incarcerated at the infamous Camp Crame before being fully exonerated. During her time as a political prisoner, she helped organize inmates, held political discussions and even conducted a 22-day hunger strike. In 1995, looking back on the turbulent time, she told the *Examiner*, "The only thing explosive about me was my mouth and my farts."

She expanded: "Filipinos laugh a lot. We laugh at our mistakes. It's one of the strengths we have. We can also fight."

And fight she did. Undeterred by her time in prison, in 1984, she co-founded Gabriela Women's Party — an organization formed after 10,000 women marched against Marcos, defying a ban on protests. That same year, Violeta also helped found Selda, an advocacy organization by and for political prisoners. Violeta also had a hand in opening two safe havens for women: the Buklod Center, geared towards sex workers, and the Batis Center for Women, which focused on female migrant workers.

Violeta finally came back to the Bay Area in 1988 and, though there was no Manilatown to return to, went straight back to work for Filipino immigrants. She worked as a social worker throughout the 1990s and remained focused on seniors and veterans, setting up food and clothing banks at two separate locations. In 1993, she co-founded the Friends of Filipino American Veterans, and in 1994, she was president of the Filipino American Human Rights Advocates.

Violeta also worked with teens on AIDS prevention and cultural empowerment. "In the curriculum," she said, "there is no cultural empowerment of other groups. How could our children have self-esteem in school when they don't see they are part of the history of America?"

Sadly, Violeta's life of service was cut short by an accident in April 2000. She was 61. At a packed memorial service at San Francisco's City Hall, tributes poured in from Mayor Willie Brown, several supervisors and a plethora of friends and associates. Supervisor Leland Yee didn't mince words:

"Anyone with the name 'Bullet,' you don't want to mess around with," Yee said. "When you lose someone like that, you lose part of your soul."

Barbara May Cameron

IN 1963, WHEN SHE WAS just 9 years old, Barbara May Cameron read an article about San Francisco. At the time, Barbara, a Hunkpapa Lakota, lived on the Standing Rock Reservation in North Dakota with her grandparents. As soon as she read about the far-away California city, she confidently informed her grandmother that, one day, she would live there. "And save the world too," she added.

Just over a decade later, Barbara made it to San Francisco and got to work. First, she co-founded Gay American Indians (GAI) alongside her friend Randy Burns. Barbara viewed GAI as both a support group for Native lesbians and gay men, and a means to carve out space for them within the wider (and whiter) LGBTQ+ community. Those pursuits carried over into her writing as well. Though she had originally trained as a photographer at Santa Fe's Institute of American Indian Arts, Barbara found her message was better conveyed through essays. Hers were personal and powerful, and she became a loudspeaker for the Indigenous gay community.

Barbara's 1981 essay "Gee, You Don't Seem Like an Indian from the Reservation" remains a searing snapshot of the struggle to survive and thrive despite marginalization. In it, she vividly describes 26 years of bearing witness to violence against her community. Remarkably, she also uses that backdrop as a means to openly discuss her own lasting trauma and the challenge of erasing color lines.

> Because of experiencing racial violence, I sometimes panic when I'm the only non-white in a roomful of whites, even if they are my closest friends; I wonder if I'll leave the room alive. The seemingly copacetic gay world of

> San Francisco becomes a mere dream after the panic leaves . . . I want to scream out my anger and disgust with myself for feeling distrustful of my white friends and I want to banish the society that has fostered those feelings of alienation.

Later, as Barbara describes working on becoming more comfortable in a white-dominated world, she wonders aloud about how she'll do that without leaving some of her "Indianness" behind. As it turns out, for the rest of her life, Barbara never lost sight of her roots and identity.

Barbara's ability to use her own life story to magnify the struggles of Native American people was hugely impactful at the time, and remains powerful today. And she did it in essay after essay, never once shying away from uncomfortable, difficult subjects. "It is inappropriate for progressive or liberal white people," she once wrote, "to expect warriors in brown armor to eradicate racism."

In her 1993 piece "Frybread in Berlin" (originally published in the fourth *In The Wind: American Indian Alaska Native Community AIDS Network* newsletter), Barbara expressed frustration over the lack of visibility permitted to people of color within the gay community. She wrote:

> In reading newspapers in the SF Bay Area, one gets the impression that the only news coming out of the IXth International Conference on AIDS is the disruptions by ACT-UP, pretending they represent the heart and soul of all AIDS activism. But . . . Alaska Soto from the Native and Indigenous AIDS Network (NIAN) addressed the closing plenary with a reading of the group statement from NIAN. The statement reflected the continued frustration and efforts by Native people to be serious participants in the international arena of HIV and AIDS.

Critical though she was about issues of inclusivity within the LGBTQ+ community, Barbara also never stopped fighting for it. Her activism was prolific. Between 1980 and '85, she helped organize the Lesbian Gay Freedom Day Parade and Celebration (the predecessor to what San Franciscans have been calling the Dyke March since 1993). And in 1981, she co-chaired the Gay Freedom Day Committee.

Though outspoken and formidable, Barbara is often remembered for her calm and respectful energy in the face of opposition. Those qualities made her a natural leader, and the positions she came to occupy reflect that.

In the late '80s, Barbara co-chaired the Lesbian Agenda for Action, an organization that used social and political action to promote lesbian visibility. During the same period, she served as vice president of the Alice B. Toklas LGBT Democratic Club. The organization's mission since 1971 has been to advocate within the Democratic party for social and economic justice, and to help elect candidates who are focused on the fight for equality.

Barbara's position facilitated new and significant political connections that raised her profile even further. She served as a delegate for Jesse Jackson's Rainbow Coalition at the 1988 Democratic National Convention. Also that year, then-Mayor Dianne Feinstein appointed Barbara to the Citizens Committee on Community Development, and the San Francisco Human Rights Commission. When Frank Jordan became mayor in 1992, he appointed her to the United Nations Commission on the Status of Women. And between 1989 and '92, Cameron was the executive director of Community United Against Violence — an organization dedicated to helping survivors of domestic violence and hate crimes.

In the end, Barbara's passion, resilience and dedication allowed her not only to become a beacon and a voice for marginalized groups in the Bay Area, but also to act as a bridge between them. Chrystos, a Native American poet and activist, once said that Barbara had given her, "a sense of dignity about my place in the world, and my right to be in that place."

Barbara May Cameron died in 2002 at the age of 47, leaving behind her partner of 21 years, Linda Boyd, and their son Rhys. She was buried in South Dakota, just outside the reservation where she was raised.

Ruth Brinker

IN 1985, AMERICA WAS IN THE MIDST of scrambling to figure out how to tackle AIDS. It was the year that Ronald Reagan was finally forced to publicly acknowledge the disease; the year of the very first International AIDS Conference; the year Rock Hudson died, leaving $250,000 behind to set up the American Foundation for AIDS Research; and the year a soft-spoken grandma named Ruth Brinker decided something must be done to assist people with HIV in the community.

At the time, fear around AIDS was at an all-time high. *Time* magazine published an article in August 1985 documenting the confusion and panic that was gripping communities nationwide. Subjects in the piece included a funeral home that refused to dress a three-year-old who had died from AIDS, firemen suddenly wary of performing mouth-to-mouth resuscitation, and a 13-year-old hemophiliac named Ryan White who was excluded from his Indiana middle school after contracting the virus from a blood transfusion.

Time reported: "The issue of whether or not AIDS can be transmitted through saliva remains medically unresolved and a focus of fear."

Ruth, a San Francisco resident, was acutely aware of these issues. After finding out that a friend of hers who was living with AIDS was also suffering from malnutrition, she took it upon herself to make sure he had regular meals to eat. At first, Ruth was a one-woman operation, making food in her home kitchen for seven neighbors in need, and delivering it in an old VW van.

"It was my very first experience with AIDS," Ruth explained in a short documentary, *The Ruth Brinker Story*. "I was absolutely shattered to see how quickly [my friend] became unable to take care of himself. And I began worrying about all the other people in the city who I knew had AIDS and wondering how they were fending. And I just felt compelled to start a meal service for them."

Ruth had long been a volunteer with Meals on Wheels, and in the mid-1980s was managing a chapter of the charity. But because recipients of Meals on Wheels were required to be over the age of 60, she knew it could not help the vast majority of AIDS patients in San Francisco. A dedicated new meal service was badly needed. Project Open Hand (POH) was born.

As word spread about Ruth's good deeds, it became apparent that demand for the new service was too great for her to handle at home. After receiving a $2,000 donation from the Zen Center, Ruth found seven volunteers to assist her. A few months later, Ruth received another, much-needed, $2,000 from the Golden Gate Business Association.

"I did the cooking and preparing with one hand, while doing Meals on Wheels with the other," she told the *San Francisco Examiner* in 1987. "All this takes determination and I get an enormous amount of pleasure out of it. When someone gets out of a hospital skeletal and in a few months has put his weight back on and tells you, 'You've saved my life,' it's a good feeling."

In addition to Ruth's organizational abilities and overriding sense of determination, one of the keys to the organization's early survival was the support of LGBTQ+ venues and groups (including the San Francisco Gay Men's Chorus) that pitched in with regular fundraisers. Often the approach to raising money was incredibly scrappy.

Between 1986 and 1988, the nonprofit's budget swelled from $70,000 to $1 million. Ruth once told *Time* magazine simply, "You have to go out and beg."

By 1987, POH was operating out of the kitchen at Trinity Episcopal Church. That year, Ruth received an award from the National AIDS Network, and the honor was effective at raising the profile of Project Open Hand. This led to assistance by philanthropist James Hormel, a $125,000 donation from Chevron and a $50,000 grant from the city for new kitchen equipment and a move to larger headquarters. By then, the extra space was desperately needed.

A year after the move, Ruth confessed that toward the end of POH's time operating out of Trinity, "people were peeling potatoes and carrots in the halls, and making sandwiches in the vestry, and the choir's robing room was our computer department."

Once in their upgraded headquarters in the Mission District, with the help of 100 volunteers' eager helping hands, POH was able to make and distribute over 2,000 meals a day, still propelled by Ruth's simple idea that food is love.

By 1989, POH was serving patients across the Bay in Alameda County. That same year, after the Loma Prieta earthquake, the project provided food to tens of thousands of residents whose houses had been destroyed. With the Bay Bridge shut down due to its partial collapse, meals were delivered to the East Bay via BART and sheer force of will.

By 1998, POH was also serving seniors all over San Francisco. Two years after that, its service expanded to people living with a variety of debilitating diseases, cancer, diabetes and heart disease included. Ruth oversaw the expansions at every stage.

Today, POH is still thriving, providing an astonishing 2,500 meals and 200 bags of groceries per day, day-after-day, and its continued success has inspired the founding of similar organizations around the world.

Ruth Marie Brinker died in 2011 at the age of 89, after enduring a series of strokes. Most of her ashes were scattered at Golden Gate Park's AIDS Memorial Grove. The outpouring after her death was enormous.

"I have walked in the Pride Parade with many, many contingents," attorney Bill Ambrunn said, "including with popular elected officials and celebrities. But it was never like the experience walking with Ruth as part of the POH contingent. All along the parade route, you could hear people crying out, 'We love you, Ruth. Thank you, Ruth.' People clapped and cheered enthusiastically for the tiny little lady waving from the car. They knew her and knew her story and loved her."

Nabila Mango

WHEN BELOVED SAN FRANCISCO drag artist Mama Ganuush first arrived in the Bay Area from Egypt in 2009, they were unemployed, unhoused and recovering from years of homophobic persecution. Ganuush sought support at the Tenderloin Health Clinic and quickly happened upon the woman they would come to call their "chosen mother."

Nabila Mango was then 65 years old, a former librarian and teacher who had pivoted into working as a therapist. The change of profession came about after a spike in anti-Arab hatred after September 11, 2001. Nabila aimed to assist at-risk people of Middle Eastern descent, but her door was open to everyone in need.

"Nabila, she saved my life when I came here," Ganuush told KQED in 2023. When Nabila offered Ganuush a room in her home, it was a direct path to getting their life on track. "I got a job, I settled down, and I became an executive in tech almost 10 years later."

It was second nature for Nabila to forge these kinds of bonds and create paths for healing. She had changed professions often throughout her life, always with a focus on building bridges between different ethnicities and cultures. Prior to becoming a therapist, Nabila taught Arabic at schools, including San Francisco City College and San Mateo's Skyline College. Her students were regularly invited to her San Mateo home to learn about Arabic music, literature and food, and to mingle with people for whom Arabic was a first language. Needless to say, this made her an enormously popular faculty member.

It was the desire to study library science that first brought Nabila to the United States at the age of 21. She emigrated from Jordan, where she had lived since she was four. Nabila had been born in Jaffa, Palestine, but when her family was forced from their homeland in 1948 after Israel was established, her family made their way to Jordan in search of refuge. Nabila's daughter, Bisan Shehadeh later noted, "Displacement was one of the greatest pains my mother carried."

Nabila adapted to American life quickly after arriving in 1965, despite some initial culture shocks. Her goals around connection were clear from the moment she arrived. While still a student at Glassboro State College in New Jersey, Nabila even visited a local ninth grade class to answer questions about life in the Middle East.

After graduation, Nabila was employed in libraries at Harvard University and the University of Chicago. She worked as a translator and contributed to the book *Kahlil Gibran: His Life and World*. (The book notes that she retrieved and translated "all the voluminous Arabic material consulted." Those translations were also consulted for Jean Gibran's 2017 book, *Kahlil Gibran: Beyond Borders*.)

In the mid-1970s, Nabila returned to her studies, completing a PhD in Persian literary history at the University of Pennsylvania. While there, she acted as an officer of the Arab-American Federation of Pennsylvania. She also served as president of the Philadelphia Chapter of the Association of Arab-American University Graduates, making regular public speaking appearances and taking part in roundtables to highlight Palestinian issues to diverse audiences.

After her time at the university, Nabila headed to California. By 1982, she and her then-husband, Saber Shehadeh, had welcomed their only daughter. Seeking a role that would enable her to stay at home, but continue with her mission, Nabila started a company to distribute books in the Arabic language. By the '90s, the business had expanded to also export computer products to Arab countries.

It was in 2000 that Nabila co-founded the project that she would become most widely recognized for: a musical collective named the Aswat Ensemble, which is still active today. Nabila, who is said to have owned one of the largest collections of Arabic music in North America, initially wanted to ensure that Palestinian folk songs were preserved. But the longer Aswat continued, the more the group expanded both its philosophy and musical style.

By 2011, Aswat included musicians and singers from the Palestinian territories, Israel, Turkey, Lebanon, Egypt, France, Morocco, Mexico, India, Jordan, Iran, Iraq and, yes, the United States. Many of the instruments utilized were traditional ones from the Middle East.

In 2017, during an interview with The *San Francisco Chronicle*, Nabila described the Aswat ethos: "We are convinced that once one has experienced the artistic richness of another culture," she said, "they are much less likely to dehumanize them by seeing them through media-propagated stereotypes."

Nabila's work with Aswat led to other important projects, including Ayadi, a nonprofit she founded to provide aid and support to low-income Bay Area Arab and Muslim families. The organization's activities included a communal dinner to feed scores of underprivileged families every Sunday. In 2012, she received a grant to develop Doorway to Islamic Civilization, a series of arts and culture workshops.

Today, Aswat Ensemble and offshoots including Aswat Youth and Aswat Women's Ensemble are all programs within Zawaya, a nonprofit for which Nabila served as executive director. Zawaya remains focused on preserving, producing and promoting Arabic arts in the Bay Area, presenting regular art shows, theatrical productions and other opportunities for community gatherings, in addition to its focus on music.

On November 13, 2023, after a long, fiercely fought battle against cancer, Nabila Mango finally left the Earth that she wanted so badly to unite. Her focus was always on community — local and global. One of her most powerful contributions to communal resistance and resilience was the preservation of Palestinian culture for generations to come.

Shortly after Nabila's death, it was her daughter who summed up Nabila's magical powers best of all:

"She planted seeds, she watered them, she tended them and they grew into beautiful things," Bisan Shehadeh told the *Chronicle*. "She made most people feel like they had a special relationship with her. That was the size of her heart."

Judy Heumann

NEVER IN HER LIFE DID SHE feel ashamed to use a wheelchair. Rather, what Judy Heumann felt most consistently throughout her life was fury at the many ways she was routinely excluded by a world that treated disabled people as second-class citizens.

"Disability isn't a tragedy," she said in 1990. "The tragedy is being excluded from contributing to society because of a narrow doorway, or lack of a diploma or job."

Judy knew all about being excluded. After losing her ability to walk in 1949 after a bout of polio at 18 months old, the New Yorker was denied a place in her local school because the administration there considered her "a fire hazard." At 9 or 10, she was permitted to join special education classes in the basement of a Brooklyn school. ("We respected each other," Judy later said of her classmates, but "in some way, even when we were that young, we all knew we were being sidelined.") In 1970, despite her being qualified to receive a teaching license, the New York City Board of Education deemed her too much of a risk to allow in classrooms.

When Judy called the ACLU for legal assistance, the 22-year-old was told that being denied a teaching license for "medical reasons" didn't count as discrimination. She was frustrated to realize that even the 1964 Civil Rights Act excluded her.

As Judy wrote in her 2020 autobiography, *Being Heumann*, "[The act is] intended to end discrimination on the basis of race, color, religion and national origin, but made no mention of disability. There was no law I could quote or legal precedent to cite . . . There were no disability rights organizations."

It was then that Judy began her lifelong work to methodically and systematically transform America for people with disabilities.

Judy's life of activism began when she decided to ignore the ACLU's assessment. Instead, she sued the Board of Education and won. Judy became the first wheelchair-using teacher in New York. In the course of that battle, she also founded and became president of Disabled in Action (DIA). The disability rights organization used protests, letter-writing campaigns, statements at public hearings and calls to public officials to make headway with their struggles. Its members absolutely refused to blend into the background.

"We didn't just come to meetings," Judy said in the 2020 documentary *Crip Camp*. "We yelled out at meetings, we challenged people."

Judy brought that energy with her to U.C. Berkeley, where she earned a master's degree in public health. In 1973, she joined the board of the Center for Independent Living (CIL), which had been founded a year earlier by Ed Roberts, the first wheelchair user to attend U.C. Berkeley. The CIL acted as a support network for people with disabilities, offering accessible transit, personal assistant referrals, and help in locating suitable housing and jobs, and even running a wheelchair repair shop. The end goal was self-sufficiency for all disabled people.

Judy's focus, as always, was turning community frustration into positive action. Her talent for doing so would become abundantly clear in April 1977, when she and around 100 other protesters staged a 24-day sit-in at the Department of Health, Education and Welfare inside San Francisco's Federal Building.

The lengthy protest was part of an effort to get Section 504 of the 1973 Rehabilitation Act signed and enacted by the Secretary of Health, Education, and Welfare. Section 504 prohibited discrimination by any organization that was receiving federal funds. (President Nixon had only signed the Rehabilitation Act after Judy and 50 other protesters shut down a major intersection of Manhattan in front of Nixon's New York headquarters.) Judy and her cohort knew that getting the measure signed would force a major change in how public transport, public buildings, schools and a variety of other institutions accommodated people with disabilities.

The sit-in was especially arduous for the protesters due to their reliance on medications, assistants and therapeutic equipment. Civil rights groups across the Bay Area rushed to offer support. The Black Panthers brought the protesters hot meals on a nightly basis. Union members, multiple civil rights organizations and key local leaders offered assistance in whatever way they could.

After a lengthy standoff — including attempts to cut off protesters' access to phones, hot water and food — Secretary of Health, Education, and Welfare Joseph Califano finally signed Section 504.

Judy and her fellow protesters knew there was still much to be done. Though on paper, Section 504 meant federally funded entities must accommodate disabled people, excuses were repeatedly made about why action would not be taken immediately. Stronger legal protections were still needed.

Judy continued working as CIL's senior deputy director. In Oakland, she co-founded the World Institute on Disability (WID) to begin advocating for disability rights around the globe. CIL also set up a new organization to handle ongoing legal matters. The Disability Rights Education and Defense Fund (DREDF) was the first legal organization run by and for people with disabilities. While fielding calls from people seeking advice on how to make their towns and cities more accessible, DREDF was also at work on a big idea to touch every corner of America in one swoop: the Americans with Disabilities Act (ADA).

It took until 1988 for the first version of the ADA to reach Congress. It failed to pass. A second version arrived in May 1989, and when it still hadn't passed 10 months later, 1,000 protesters descended on Washington, D.C., to make their voices heard. Scores of disabled activists dropped to the ground and literally dragged themselves up the 83 inaccessible steps of the Capitol building. It was an image that lawmakers wouldn't soon forget. On July 26, 1990, President George H.W. Bush finally signed the ADA into law.

Judy never stopped advocating for people with disabilities, and by the time of her death in 2023, at the age of 75, her impact was seismic.

As she wrote in her 2021 book, *Rolling Warrior*: "All we did was refuse to believe that we were the problem."

ACKNOWLEDGMENTS

Thank you to Elaine Katzenberger, Stacey Lewis and City Lights — the coolest publisher on Earth — for believing in this project and gently guiding me through the publishing process for the first time. It has been a dream come true.

Thank you to Adrienne Simms for the beautiful illustrations that so gracefully honor each and every woman in this book and bring them to such vivid life, even when images of some of the women I profiled were entirely lost to history. I couldn't have imagined more fitting portraits.

This book would not have been possible without the long-term support of KQED, in particular the entire KQED Arts & Culture team, past and present. I owe a huge debt of gratitude to Sarah Hotchkiss, Gabe Meline and Nastia Voynovskaya for their thoughtful editing skills and ceaseless encouragement to keep going, even through the bleakest months of the pandemic shutdown. Special thanks to Becca Kao for their design work on the original *Rebel Girls From Bay Area History* online series. Thanks also to all of the donors that keep public media alive.

A deep and enduring thank-you to the dedicated staff of libraries and archives across the Bay Area that have shared their time, materials and enthusiasm with me over the last eight years. Those organizations include: the San Francisco History Center, the California Historical Society, the African American Museum and Library at Oakland, the GLBT Historical Society Museum & Archives, U.C. Berkeley's Bancroft Library, and the Sacramento History Museum. Special thanks to Erika Surat Andersen for telling me all about your grandmother, Kartar Dhillon, and to PJ Singh for connecting me with Erika in the first place. Without you all, I would be lost.

Love and thanks to my most supportive best friends, Rania Adwan and Nicole Newsom, who have been in this with me for literally decades. One of you attended one of my speaking events in the midst of a crippling bout of vertigo and one of you stopped me from accidentally driving off a cliff on the way to Bodie to do research. For this and so much more, you both rule.

Eternal thanks to my partner in crime DBC Kanel, who, among many other kindnesses, fed me when I was too bogged down in edits to feed myself. I love you. Put it on the stairs.

Thank you to Mavemond, my parents. Mavis, you have encouraged my writing in every conceivable way for my entire life. None of this would have happened without you. Raymond, you taught me to how to stand my ground in every facet of my life. May this book offer some consolation for my fiscally irresponsible refusal to become a lawyer.

Thank you, San Francisco, for the Mission District and making me fall in love with history in the first place. You are the most magical city in the world.

Thank you to each and every woman in this book. I will continue shouting your names as long as there is breath in my body.